Writing the Critical Essay

The
Iraq War

An OPPOSING  VIEWPOINTS® Guide

Lauri S. Friedman, *Book Editor*

**OPPOSING
VIEWPOINTS®
SERIES**

GREENHAVEN PRESS
A part of Gale, Cengage Learning

GALE
CENGAGE Learning™

Detroit • New York • San Francisco • New Haven, Conn • Waterville, Maine • London

Christine Nasso, *Publisher*
Elizabeth Des Chenes, *Managing Editor*

For more information, contact:
Greenhaven Press
27500 Drake Rd.
Farmington Hills, MI 48331-3535
Or you can visit our Internet site at gale.cengage.com

LIBRARY OF CONGRESS CATALOGING-IN-PUBLICATION DATA

The Iraq War / Lauri S. Friedman, book editor.
    p. cm. — (Writing the critical essay, an opposing viewpoints guide)
Includes bibliographical references and index.
ISBN-13: 978-0-7377-4037-0 (hardcover)
  1. Iraq War, 2003—Juvenile literature. 2. United States—Politics and government—2001—Juvenile literature. I. Friedman, Lauri S.
DS79.763.I76 2008
956.7044'3—dc22
                                       2008002155

Printed in the United States of America
1 2 3 4 5 6 7 12 11 10 09 08

CONTENTS

Examining the state of writing and how it is taught in the United States was the official purpose of the National Commission on Writing in America's Schools and Colleges. The commission, made up of teachers, school administrators, business leaders, and college and university presidents, released its first report in 2003. "Despite the best efforts of many educators," commissioners argued, "writing has not received the full attention it deserves." Among the findings of the commission was that most fourth-grade students spent less than three hours a week writing, that three-quarters of high school seniors never receive a writing assignment in their history or social studies classes, and that more than 50 percent of first-year students in college have problems writing error-free papers. The commission called for a "cultural sea change" that would increase the emphasis on writing for both elementary and secondary schools. These conclusions have made some educators realize that writing must be emphasized in the curriculum. As colleges are demanding an ever-higher level of writing proficiency from incoming students, schools must respond by making students more competent writers. In response to these concerns, the SAT, an influential standardized test used for college admissions, required an essay for the first time in 2005.

Books in the Writing the Critical Essay: An Opposing Viewpoints Guide series use the patented Opposing Viewpoints format to help students learn to organize ideas and arguments and to write essays using common critical writing techniques. Each book in the series focuses on a particular type of essay writing—including expository, persuasive, descriptive, and narrative—that students learn while being taught both the five-paragraph essay as well as longer pieces of writing that have an opinionated focus. These guides include everything necessary to help students research, outline, draft, edit, and ultimately write successful essays across the curriculum, including essays for the SAT.

Using Opposing Viewpoints

This series is inspired by and builds upon Greenhaven Press's acclaimed Opposing Viewpoints series. As in the parent series, each book in the Writing the Critical Essay series focuses on a timely and controversial social issue that provides lots of opportunities for creating thought-provoking essays. The first section of each volume begins with a brief introductory essay that provides context for the opposing viewpoints that follow. These articles are chosen for their accessibility and clearly stated views. The thesis of each article is made explicit in the article's title and is accentuated by its pairing with an opposing or alternative view. These essays are both models of persuasive writing techniques and valuable research material that students can mine to write their own informed essays. Guided reading and discussion questions help lead students to key ideas and writing techniques presented in the selections.

The second section of each book begins with a preface discussing the format of the essays and examining characteristics of the featured essay type. Model five-paragraph and longer essays then demonstrate that essay type. The essays are annotated so that key writing elements and techniques are pointed out to the student. Sequential, step-by-step exercises help students construct and refine thesis statements; organize material into outlines; analyze and try out writing techniques; write transitions, introductions, and conclusions; and incorporate quotations and other researched material. Ultimately, students construct their own compositions using the designated essay type.

The third section of each volume provides additional research material and writing prompts to help the student. Additional facts about the topic of the book serve as a convenient source of supporting material for essays. Other features help students go beyond the book for their research. Like other Greenhaven Press books, each book in the Writing the Critical Essay series includes bibliographic listings of relevant periodical articles, books, Web sites, and organizations to contact.

Writing the Critical Essay: An Opposing Viewpoints Guide will help students master essay techniques that can be used in any discipline.

The War's Effect on Life in Iraq

The Iraq War is among the most pressing foreign and domestic policy issues facing America today. It is a multifaceted problem spanning social, economic, international, political, and militaristic realms. Debates are frequent over everything from the cost of the war, to whether the war was undertaken justly, to Iraq's place in the global war on terror, to what timetable, if any, should be set for bringing U.S. troops back home. One issue that is passionately debated can be summed up in a single question: "Are Iraqis better off now than they were before the war?" A way of answering this question is to explore the humanitarian situation in Iraq and assess whether the U.S. invasion has positively or negatively affected the lives of the Iraqi people.

From some perspectives, the invasion and overthrow of Saddam Hussein vastly improved the lives of the Iraqi people. Under Saddam, Iraqis lived in a police state under military rule; they were not free to vote, read uncensored news, or travel to unapproved destinations. Since the U.S. invasion, however, Iraqis have inched closer to a democratic state. In January 2005, for example, they held the first free elections in the nation's history. At least 8 million Iraqis, or roughly 60 percent of the eligible voting population, turned out to cast their votes in the historic election. Of the election, interim prime minister Iyad Allawi said, "This is a historic moment for Iraq, a day when Iraqis can hold their heads high because they are challenging the terrorists and starting to write their future with their own hands."[1] Others point to successes such as the training of an Iraqi police force, the death of al Qaeda in Iraq leader Abu Musab al-Zarqawi in June 2006, and the drafting of an Iraqi constitution as proof that Iraq is on the road to becoming a better nation as a result of the war.

Many people believe that the invasion of Iraq and overthrow of Saddam Hussein has improved the Iraqi people's lives.

But examples of how Iraq has changed for the worse seem painfully plentiful. It is now one of the most violent countries on the planet. In 2005, according to the National Counterterrorism Center's *Country Reports on Terrorism, 2005,* Iraq was the scene of so many terrorist attacks that it accounted for more than 30 percent of the worldwide total and 55 percent of the world's fatalities from terrorist attacks (approximately eighty-three hundred deaths). Indeed, more than 3,500 attacks were perpetrated in Iraq in just that year. Most often, suicide, car, or other types of bombs were intended to cause chaos and disrupt the rebuilding efforts of the country, damage infrastructure, or cause social upheaval and pit Iraq's various ethnicities against each other. Violence only worsened in Iraq during 2006, when terrorist attacks increased by more than 90 percent. According to the 2006 version of the National Counterterrorism Center's report, Iraq accounted for 45 percent of the more than 14,000 terrorist incidents worldwide, and for 65 percent of deaths from terrorism worldwide—this resulted in more than 13,000 civilian deaths due to terrorist attacks in 2006.

In addition to death from terrorism, thousands and thousands of Iraqis have died as a result of the U.S. military effort. It is difficult to determine exactly how many Iraqis have been killed in the war because the Department of Defense does not count civilian deaths in its casualty reports. Independent studies have attempted to ascertain the number of dead from the war, and these range in their estimates. A 2006 study funded by the Massachusetts Institute of Technology put the number of dead Iraqi civilians as high as 655,000. Another study, published in the British journal the *Lancet*, put the count around 100,000. Iraq Body Count, an organization that pulls from media reports, hospital and morgue reports, and figures published by nongovernmental organizations working in Iraq, estimates that between 71,000 and 78,000 have perished. These numbers seem especially high when one realizes that prior to the U.S. invasion in 2003, Iraq had a mortality rate of only about 5.5 people per 1,000 per year (the United States has a mortality rate of about 8.167 deaths per 1,000 per year).

Indeed, the increase in violence, chaos, and instability appears to have worsened the Iraqi quality of life in several other ways. Murders, kidnappings, and bombings have become so commonplace that many Iraqis report being afraid to leave their homes. Violence and war have destroyed the country's infrastructure, resulting in power shortages, fuel shortages, and a lack of clean water. For example, in October 2006 utility service in Baghdad reached record low levels. Residents of Baghdad received an average of 2.4 hours of electricity, compared to an average of 16 to 24 hours of electricity before the war began. Medical care is also widely unavailable, as facilities lack adequate supplies and many physicians have been forced to leave the country.

For all of these reasons, Iraq has been ranked second on a list of failed states of 2007 published jointly by the Fund for Peace and *Foreign Policy* magazine. Indeed, Iraq was labeled as the world's second-most unstable country, ahead of war-torn or poverty-stricken nations such as Somalia, Congo, Afghanistan, Haiti, and North Korea. For this reason there are many Iraqis who believe life was better for them under the dictatorship of Saddam Hussein. They may have not been free, but they were safe and could lead normal lives, as one Iraqi named Hanna Milla believes. Of the time before the invasion, Milla says, "It was, my God, wonderful. I used to go out. I used to shop."[2]

But others say that the violence and upheaval in Iraq are growing pains on the way to freedom, security, and democracy. In fact, in a July 4, 2007, speech delivered to

Unrest and terrorism continue as the Iraq War persists. Iraqi civilians are often the target of continued violence.

the West Virginia Air National Guard, President George W. Bush discussed another nation that endured violence and bloodshed on the road to peace, stability, and freedom. "Our first Independence Day celebration took place in a midst of a war—a bloody and difficult struggle that would not end for six more years before America finally secured her freedom. More than two [centuries] later, it is hard to imagine the Revolutionary War coming out any other way—but at the time, America's victory was far from certain," Bush said of the American Revolution. He likened that struggle to the current one in Iraq, saying, "However difficult the fight is in Iraq, we must win it—we must succeed for our own sake."[3]

Whether the war has benefited the Iraqi people and whether it will truly result in a free, safe, and democratic state remains to be seen. The humanitarian situation in Iraq is just one of the issues explored in the articles and model essays included in *Writing the Critical Essay: An Opposing Viewpoints Guide: The Iraq War*. Model essays and viewpoints expose readers to the basic arguments made about Iraq and help them develop tools to craft their own essays on the subject.

Notes

1. Quoted in PBS.org, "Millions of Iraqis Vote in First Free Election," January 31, 2005. www.pbs.org/newshour/extra/features/jan-june05/iraq_1-31.pdf.

2. Quoted in Ellen Knickmeyer, "Iraqi Women See Little but Darkness," *Washington Post*, October 15, 2005, p. A14.

3. "President Bush Celebrates Independence Day with West Virginia Air National Guard," The White House, July 4, 2007. www.whitehouse.gov/news/releases/2007/07/20070704.html.

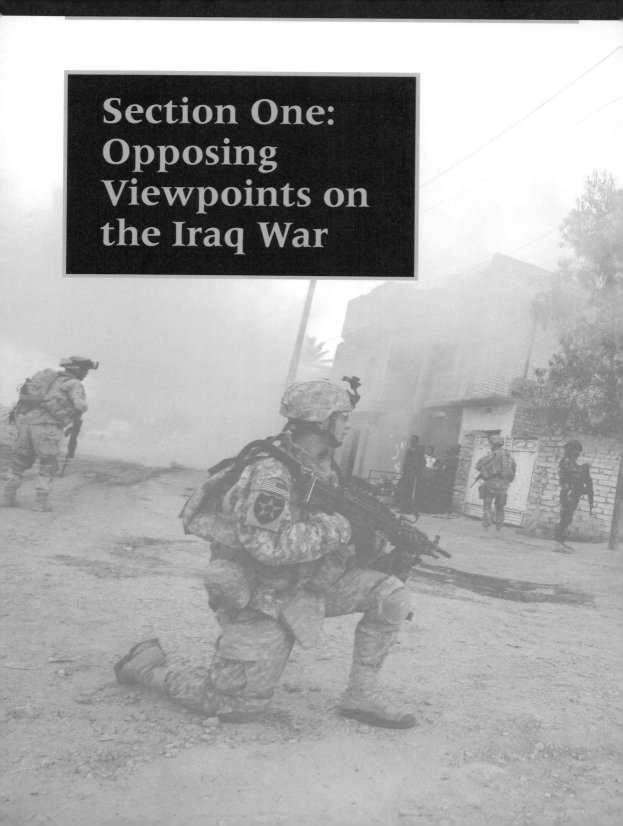

Section One: Opposing Viewpoints on the Iraq War

The Iraq War Has Helped Fight Terrorism

Dick Cheney

In the following essay NBC's Tim Russert interviews Vice President Dick Cheney about whether the war in Iraq has helped reduce terrorism. Cheney maintains that it has, citing the removal of former Iraqi dictator Saddam Hussein as a key point of progress. Cheney claims that Hussein rewarded the families of suicide bombers and sought weapons of mass destruction to use against the United States and its allies. Cheney also challenges claims that the war in Iraq is tangential to the war on terror, arguing that America's success in Iraq will be a blow to terrorists all over the world. Likewise, he warns, failure there will embolden terrorists. Cheney acknowledges that the terrorist insurgency in Iraq has gone on longer than expected but concludes that without the war in Iraq, the terrorist problem would have been much worse.

Cheney is the forty-sixth vice president of the United States. Russert is the Washington Bureau Chief for NBC News and hosts *Tim Russert*, a weekly interview program on CNBC.

Consider the following questions:

1. What percent of Americans believe the war in Iraq has created more terrorists, as reported by Russert?
2. According to Cheney, what would the world be like if Saddam Hussein were still in power?
3. What is key to victory in Iraq, in Cheney's opinion?

Dick Cheney and Tim Russert, "NBC News," in *Meet the Press*, September 10, 2006.

Q. Mr. Vice President, tomorrow marks the fifth anniversary of September 11th, and in many way marks the beginning of the war on terrorism. Three years ago, the Secretary of Defense Donald Rumsfeld wondered out loud, are we creating or recruiting more terrorists than we are killing? What do you think? Five years later, are there more terrorists now than there were five years ago?

Significant Progress in Reducing Terrorism

A. It's hard to say, Tim, and hard to put a precise number on it. It's changing and evolving to some extent. We've done enormous damage to al Qaeda, to the leadership of Al Qaeda. We've captured and killed hundreds of their senior people. By the same token, you've got wannabe organizations, Al Qaeda organizations out there now that have only a remote connection to the center. The groups, for example that the Brits have uncovered recently. These are second-generation immigrants to the U.K. These are not people living in the Middle East, or who have grown up terror training camps in Afghanistan the way the original group did. So it is changing and evolving. On the other hand, I think we've also made—just say, I think we've made significant progress.

The removal of former Iraqi dictator Saddam Hussein (center, right) has been an important milestone for the success of the Iraq war.

Q. It's interesting. Here's what the American people said in a recent poll: Is the U.S. involvement in Iraq or Afghanistan creating more terrorists or eliminating terrorists. And look at that, overwhelmingly, 54 percent, a clear majority, believe we are creating more terrorists.

A. I can't buy that. I think you've got to look at what's happening in Afghanistan and Iraq in terms of where we were five years ago and where we are today. Take Afghanistan: Afghanistan was governed by the Taliban, one of the worst regimes in modern times, terribly dictatorial, terribly discriminatory towards women. There were training camps in Afghanistan training thousands of Al Qaeda terrorists; all of those camps today are shut down. The Taliban are no longer in power. There is a democratically elected President, a democratically elected parliament, a new constitution, and American-trained Afghan security forces—and NATO now—actively in the fight against the remnants of the Taliban. We are much better off today because Afghanistan is not the safe haven for terror that it was on 9/11. . . .

> ## Iraq Has Been Key to the War on Terror
>
> There's more than one front in this war against these radicals and extremists. And, obviously, the toughest threat of all is in Iraq. In that country, we removed a cruel dictator who harbored terrorists, paid the families of Palestinian suicide bombers, invaded his neighbors, defied the United Nations Security Council, pursued and used weapons of mass destruction. The world is better off without Saddam Hussein in power.
>
> Speech by President George W. Bush, President Bush Celebrates Independence Day with West Virginia Air National Guard, July 4, 2007. http://www.whitehouse.gov/news/releases/2007/07/20070704.html.

The War in Iraq Is Key to the War on Terror

Q. And yet if you ask the American people, is the war in Iraq a part of the war on terror, this is what they now say: 46 percent, yes; 53 percent, a majority, say it is not part of the war on terror.

A. Well, I beg to differ. Let's walk through it. Look at where we are in Iraq today. I do think we've made major progress. Five years ago, Saddam Hussein was in power in Iraq. Iraq was a major state sponsor of terror. Saddam Hussein was providing payments, bonuses to the families of suicide bombers. He had a history of starting two wars. He had produced and used weapons of mass destruction. It was one of the worst regimes of modern times. We moved aggressively against Saddam Hussein. Today you've got Saddam in jail where he's being prosecuted for having butchered thousands of people.[1] You've a democratically elected government. There have been three nationwide elections, there has been a new constitution written. We've got almost 300,000 Iraqis now trained and equipped in the security forces. And we are—that's significant progress by anybody's standards. It's still difficult. It's still obviously major, major work to do ahead of us. But the fact is, the world is much better off today with Saddam Hussein out of power.

A Major Sponsor of Terror Eliminated

Think where we would be if he was still there. He would be sitting on top of a big pile of cash because he would have $65 and $70 oil. He would by now have taken down the sanctions because he had already with the corrupted Oil for Food Program, nearly destroyed them when he was still in power. He would be a major state sponsor of terror.

We also would have a situation where he would resumed his WMD programs. . . . So to suggest somehow that the world is not better off by having Saddam in jail I think is just dead wrong. . . .

A Turning Point for Terrorism

Q. I want to go back to May 30th, 2005 when you said to the American people and to the world, "I think the level of activity in Iraq that we see today from military standpoint, I think, will clearly decline. I think they are in the last throes, if you will, of the insurgency."

Since that time, Mr. Vice President, look at this, between the beginning of the war and May 30th when you made that statement we had 1,656 deaths in Iraq.

---

1. Saddam Hussein was executed in December 2006.

Iraqis Are Optimistic About Their Future

A 2007 poll of Iraqis found that the majority of Iraqis believe that though Iraq is struggling to find its way, it will not succumb to sectarian violence.

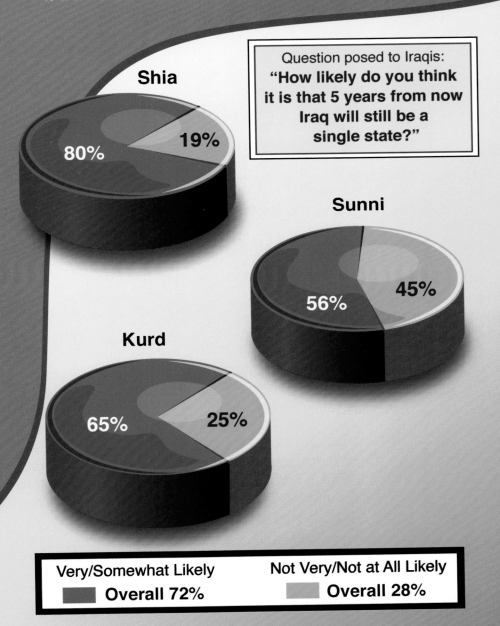

Shia

80%   19%

Question posed to Iraqis:
"How likely do you think it is that 5 years from now Iraq will still be a single state?"

Sunni

56%   45%

Kurd

65%   25%

Very/Somewhat Likely
Overall 72%

Not Very/Not at All Likely
Overall 28%

Taken from: *Iraq Index Tracking Variables of Reconstruction & Security in Post-Saddam Iraq,* Brookings Institution, August 6, 2007. http://www3.brookings.edu/fp/saban/iraq/index.pdf.

Vice president Dick Cheney believes the War in Iraq has reduced terrorism, and America's success will one day end terrorism worldwide.

There are now a thousand more American servicemen. There are 7,500 more wounded and injured. There are 20,000 more dead Iraqis. Wasn't it a flat-out mistake to say we are in the last throes of the insurgency?

A. I think there's no question, Tim, that the insurgency has gone on longer and been more difficult than I had anticipated. I'll be the first to admit that. But I also think when we look back on this period of time 10 years from now, and this is the context in which I made that statement last year, that 2005 will have been the turning point, because that's the point at which the Iraqis stepped up, and established their own political process, wrote a constitution, held three national elections and basically took on the responsibility for their own fate and their future.

And as I mentioned before, in Afghanistan, in Pakistan, in Saudi Arabia and in Iraq, the key to victory is for us to be able to get the locals into the fight. The United States can't do it all by itself. It can't be only U.S. security forces fighting in Iraq or Afghanistan. They've got to be willing to step up and take on the responsibility for their own fate. But they are doing it. And it's absolutely essential that we complete that mission.

If Not for United States in Iraq, Terrorism Would Be Far Worse

Now, is it tough and difficult? Absolutely. No doubt about it. You regret every single casualty. I visit with the families. We spend time with the wounded when they come back. I visit with the troops every chance I get. It's the toughest thing the President has to do. But it is absolutely the right thing to do, Tim, because if we weren't there, if Saddam Hussein were still in power, the situation would be far worse than it is today.

You'd have a man who had a demonstrated capacity for violence, who'd started two wars, who had, in fact, been involved with weapons of mass destruction, who had every intention of going back to it when the sanctions were lifted. And by this point, especially with [Iranian president Mahmoud] Ahmadinejad, living next door in Iran, pursuing nuclear weapons, there is no doubt in my mind that if Saddam Hussein was still in power, he would have a very robust program underway to try to do exactly the same thing. The world is better off because Saddam Hussein is in jail instead of in power in Baghdad. It was the right thing to do, and if we had to do it over again we would do exactly the same thing.

Analyze the essay:

1. Cheney is the vice president of the United States. Does knowing his position influence the weight you give his argument? Why or why not? Explain your reasoning.

2. Cheney claims that the war in Iraq has done enormous damage to al Qaeda. How do you think Doug Bandow, author of the following essay, would respond to this claim?

The Iraq War Has Increased Terrorism

Doug J. Bandow

In the following essay author Doug J. Bandow argues that the war in Iraq has increased the number of terrorists that want to hurt America and its allies. He explains that because the war in Iraq has been seen as an unjust war in which many thousands of innocent civilians have been killed, it has become a prime example for terrorists of why they should hate the United States. In this way, it feeds their narrative of why terrorism is just and makes it easier to recruit new terrorists. Furthermore, because the war has been so mishandled, al Qaeda has been able to regroup and spread around the globe—and the United States has been unable to fight them properly because it is bogged down in Iraq. For all of these reasons, Bandow concludes the war in Iraq has worsened the terrorist problem and urges the United States to leave Iraq immediately.

Bandow is a former columnist with Copley News Service and senior fellow at the Cato Institute, a libertarian think tank. He served as a special assistant to President Ronald Reagan and as a senior policy analyst in the 1980 Reagan for President campaign. He is also a columnist for Antiwar.com, where this essay was originally published.

Consider the following questions:

1. What does the author mean when he likens George W. Bush to an orphan who kills his parents?
2. In what way is Iraq providing a "real-time, authentic 'jihad' experience" for those who want to be terrorists?
3. What does the word "metastasis" mean in the context of the viewpoint?

Douglas J. Bandow, "Fight Terrorism: Get Out of Iraq," Antiwar.com, April 27, 2007.

As the conflict in Iraq has worsened, a majority of Americans has come to believe that the war was a mistake. There were no WMDs to seize. There was no operational relationship with al-Qaeda to disrupt. There was no cohesive, democratic Iraqi nation to reclaim.

In short, the war was a terrible mistake. . . .

Iraq Was Never Part of the War on Terror

President George W. Bush has tried to tie Iraq more broadly to the fight against terrorism. He criticized Democrats for seeking an exit from Iraq, claiming: "The consequences of failure would be death and destruction in the Middle East and here in America. To protect our citizens at home, we must defeat the terrorists."

Listening to the president warning of death and destruction flowing from failure in Iraq brings to mind the man who murders his parents and then throws himself on the

Critics of the war in Iraq say it has encouraged even more militants to resort to terrorism to fight what they feel is an unjust war.

The War in Iraq Has Increased Terrorism Around the World

According to a study conducted by *Mother Jones* magazine, terrorism (both number of attacks and fatalities from those attacks) has increased worldwide since the invasion of Iraq in 2003. Globally there has been on average a 607 percent rise in the number of attacks and 237 percent rise in the fatality rate.

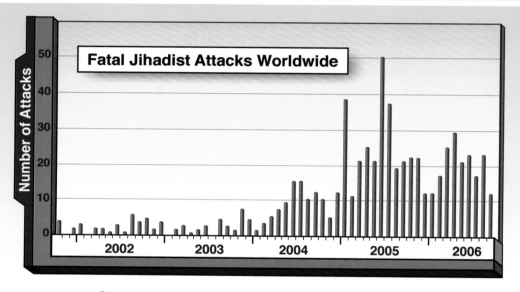

Taken from: "The Iraq Effect: War Has Increased Terrorism Sevenfold," *Mother Jones*, March 2007. www.motherjones.com/news/featurex/2007/03/aftermath.html.

court's mercy as an orphan. President Bush's decision to invade Iraq turned that nation into a cauldron of chaos and violence, fomented by a murderous mix of domestic insurgents and foreign terrorists. So now, the president argues, we must stay to suppress those same domestic insurgents and foreign terrorists.

There's just one, minor problem with the president's argument. It's not true. Even America's closest ally, Great Britain, has acknowledged the obvious. Helen Liddell, Britain's ambassador to Australia and former cabinet member, recently opined: "We have never seen Iraq as part of the war on terror." As she explained, "Certainly we are engaged in a war on the streets in Iraq against terrorism, but our raison d'etre for our involvement in Iraq has not been about terrorism."

Iraq Spawns Terrorism

It is bad enough that a war now justified as fighting terrorism does not fight terrorism. But it is worse: Iraq is creating terrorism. The conflict is creating another grievance that makes more people hate America and encourages more people to take up arms against the U.S. Iraq also is providing a convenient terrorist battleground, putting tens of thousands of Americans in reach of jihadist thugs who otherwise would remain an ocean away from the U.S.

The American people apparently understand. A new *Washington Post*–NBC poll finds that 57 percent of Americans believe that "the war on terrorism can be a success without the United States winning the war in Iraq." Indeed, to better fight terrorism we must leave Iraq. . . .

Iraq Fed the Terrorist Narrative

The invasion and occupation of Iraq have made the [terrorist] problem worse, much worse. Daniel Benjamin of the Brookings Institution testified before the House Armed Services Committee [in 2007] that "the invasion of Iraq, gave the jihadists an unmistakable boost. Terrorism is about advancing a narrative and persuading a targeted audience to believe it. Although leading figures in the American administration have often spoken of the terrorists' ideology of hatred, U.S. actions have too often lent inadvertent confirmation to the terrorists' narrative." In particular, "in the context of the culture of grievance that exists in much of the Muslim world, the extremists' narrative has had a profound resonance. Through their violence, the jihadists have also created a drama of the faith

The Iraq War Has Spread Terrorism Like a Cancer

"The misguided war in Iraq has metastasized and spread terrorism like cancer around the world."

Statement by Senator Edward M. Kennedy, "New National Intelligence Estimate Determines that the misguided war has 'metastasized and spread' terrorism," September 23, 2006. http://kennedy.senate.gov/newsroom/press_release.cfm?id=ff5e05ad-8e48-447f-a015-c3ef25303548.

Some say the Iraq War has inspired even more terrorists to join al-Qaeda, the terrorist organization led by Osama bin Laden.

that disaffected Muslims around the world can watch on television and the Internet."

London's Royal Institute for International Affairs, or Chatham House, reached a similar conclusion: "There is no doubt that the situation over Iraq has imposed particular difficulties for the UK, and for the wider coalition against terrorism. It gave a boost to the al-Qaeda network's propaganda, recruitment and fundraising, caused a major split in the coalition, provided an ideal targeting and training area for al-Qaeda-linked terrorists."

Islamists make similar points. Lebanese Grand Ayatollah Mohammed Hussein Fadlallah charged that "the method the American administration has used in the war against terror may have complicated the situation even more. . . . The occupation of Iraq has increased acts of terrorism against the U.S. and everyone going along with it, including the Iraqis themselves."

The War in Iraq Allowed al-Qaeda to Regroup

Indeed, though al-Qaeda has been damaged, the organization is recovering. Indeed, reports the *Financial Times*: "Al-Qaeda is reaching out from its base in Pakistan to turn militant Islamist groups in the Middle East and Africa into franchises charged with intensifying attacks on western targets, according to European officials and terrorism specialists. The development could see radical groups use al-Qaeda expertise to switch their attention from local targets to western interests in their countries and abroad."

Al-Qaeda is drawing particular strength from new, local groups that have sprung up in the aftermath of the Iraq war. For instance, [Iraqi terrorist leader] Ayman al-Zawahiri last year talked of a merger between al-Qaeda and an Algerian Salafist Group known as Call and Combat—apparently responsible for two recent bombings in that nation. A similar alliance might be in the offing with the Libyan Islamic Fighting Group, heretofore most known for seeking to overthrow Libyan dictator Muammar Gadhafi.

Three Kinds of New Terrorists Have Been Born

But our problem runs far beyond al-Qaeda. Benjamin Friedman argues that the Iraq war has spawned three new terrorist clusters. "The first group is comprised of self-starters, also often called 'home-grown terrorists'." These are the local killers in Madrid and London, Bali and Jakarta. Friedman adds, "These are individuals who may have very little connection to al-Qaeda or other preexisting groups, but they have been won over by the ideas of Osama bin Laden and his followers."

Iraq appears to have been one of the factors motivating these terrorists. Even a few individuals carrying out a few successful attacks have done great harm. Moreover, writes Friedman: "We should also not make the mistake of believing that terrorists who begin as self-starters will not find the connections, training and resources they seek. It is now widely accepted that the July 7, 2005 Tube bombings in London were carried out with guidance and support from jihadists in Pakistan, including possibly al-Qaeda members, who the operatives may have met during visits."

The second category Friedman points to are foreign fighters, most of whom were radicalized by the Iraq conflict. Separate studies by Saudi Nawaf Obeid and Israeli Reuven Paz reached the same conclusion: most of these imported terrorists were not previously active in jihadist circles. They are new recruits, drawn by the war. But they might not stop with Iraq. These terrorists, worries Friedman, "could become the vanguard of a new generation of jihadists, much as the veterans of the fighting in Afghanistan in the 1980s and 1990s were the founding generation of al-Qaeda."

Perhaps most fearsome is the emergence of Friedman's third group, Iraqi jihadists. Iraqis have largely taken over al-Qaeda in Iraq. Worries Friedman: "According to some reputable sources, there could be more than 15,000 in their ranks. The chaos in Iraq has allowed for extensive training and development in various terrorist tactics and urban warfare, including increasingly proficient use of improvised explosive devices." The Iraqi jihadists assert as much. Said Abu Omar al-Baghdadi, head of an Iraqi-based, al-Qaeda-linked organization, earlier this month, "From the military point of view, one of the [enemy] devils was right in saying that if Afghanistan was a school of terror, then Iraq is a university of terrorism."

Iraq Has Spread Terrorism Around the Globe

This school's foreign graduates have begun to bleed out around the world, particularly Europe and the Mideast. Equally bad is the diffusion of terrorist knowledge. Writes Friedman: "The proliferation of such tactics—thanks to traveling fighters and information-sharing via the Internet—has made it likely that the style of urban warfare tactics will likely be exported to distant regions." Iraq is providing "a real-time, authentic 'jihad' experience which is grooming a new generation of committed fighters," he concludes.

We already might have glimpsed the future: "metastasis," as Friedman puts it. More than a score of failed plots in Europe, the arrest of apparent conspirators in Australia, varying threats in South Asia and Southeast

Asia. Moreover, argues Friedman, "The implications in the Middle East/Persian Gulf region of so much jihadist activity in Iraq are ominous," with attacks and threats spreading to Arab countries once free of terrorism....

The War in Iraq Helps the Terrorist Cause

If I believed in conspiracies, I would assume that George W. Bush was a jihadist plant, someone converted long ago to fundamentalist Islam and turned into a "sleeper" agent to be activated at the moment calculated to do America the most harm. That moment came obviously with Bush's election. His needless and heedless war in Iraq has done much to generate terrorism: created a living recruiting poster, spawned a variety of new terrorists, provided a national training ground, and placed tens of thousands of Americans within easy reach of ruthless killers. Osama bin Laden couldn't ask for much more.

But I'm not a conspiracy theorist, so I assume that a toxic mix of arrogance, ignorance, and incompetence is what caused the Bush administration to unintentionally give the terrorists so much help. Any policy of continued occupation in Iraq guarantees more terrorists and more terrorism around the world. If Americans want to defeat terrorism, America must withdraw from Iraq. Until the U.S. does so, the problem of terrorism will continue to worsen.

Analyze the essay:

1. To make his argument, Bandow quotes from a variety of authors, experts, and statesmen. List everyone he quotes, along with their qualification and the nature of their comments. How did these voices lend legitimacy to the essay?

2. Bandow closes his essay by saying that if he believed in conspiracy, he would assume President George W. Bush had been planted, or been put in power by, terrorists. What does he mean by this? Did you think this was an effective way to conclude this essay? Why or why not?

The Situation in Iraq Is Improving

John McCain

John McCain is a Republican senator from Arizona and a candidate in the 2008 presidential election. In the following essay he argues that the situation in Iraq is much better than media reports would have Americans believe. He says for the first time in years, Iraqi markets are safer and roads are more secure. Furthermore, U.S. and Iraqi forces are working together as never before to fight terrorists and reduce crime. The Iraqi police force has also been significantly built up, says McCain. He interprets these as positive signs that Iraq is finally on the road to recovery, and he urges the United States not to give up on Iraq just as progress is finally beginning to be made.

Consider the following questions:

1. How does McCain say his most recent visit to Iraq differed from previous visits? List at least three examples.
2. What is one way in which U.S. troops have made Iraqi markets safer than they used to be?
3. How many joint U.S.-Iraqi police stations have been established in Baghdad, as reported by McCain?

I just returned from my fifth visit to Iraq since 2003— and my first since Gen. David Petraeus's new strategy [of bringing Iraq under control] has started taking effect. For the first time, our delegation was able to drive, not

John McCain, "The War You're Not Reading About," *Washington Post*, April 8, 2007, p. B07. Copyright © 2007 The Washington Post Company. Reproduced by permission of the author.

use helicopters, from the airport to downtown Baghdad. For the first time, we met with Sunni tribal leaders in Anbar province who are working with American and Iraqi forces to combat al-Qaeda. For the first time, we visited Iraqi and American forces deployed in a joint security station in Baghdad—an integral part of the new strategy. We held a news conference to discuss what we saw: positive signs, underreported in the United States, that are reason for cautious optimism.

I observed that our delegation "stopped at a local market, where we spent well over an hour, shopping and talking with the local people, getting their views and ideas about different issues of the day." Markets in Baghdad have faced devastating terrorist attacks. A car bombing at Shorja in February [2007], for example, killed 137 people. Today the market still faces occasional sniper attacks,

Iraqi markets and roads are becoming safer and more secure due to U.S. and Iraqi forces working together to improve the conditions in Iraq.

but it is safer than it used to be. One innovation of the new strategy is closing markets to vehicles, thereby precluding car bombs that kill so many and garner so much media attention. Petraeus understandably wanted us to see this development.

Good News About Iraq Is Underreported

I went to Iraq to gain a firsthand view of the progress in this difficult war, not to celebrate any victories. No one has been more critical of sunny progress reports that defied realities in Iraq. In 2003, after my first visit, I argued for more troops to provide the security necessary for political development. I disagreed with statements characterizing the insurgency as a "few dead-enders" or being in its "last

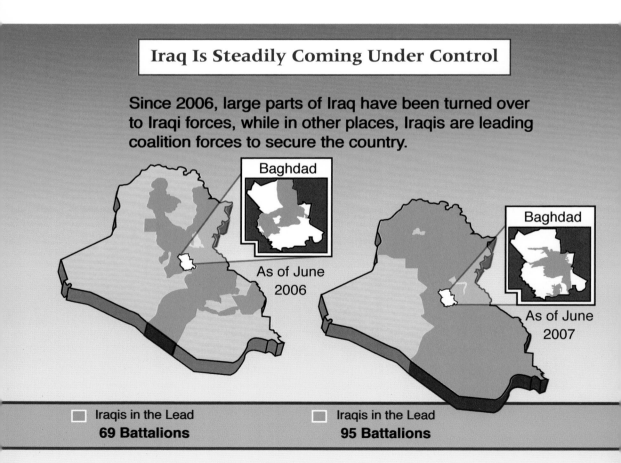

Iraq Is Steadily Coming Under Control

Since 2006, large parts of Iraq have been turned over to Iraqi forces, while in other places, Iraqis are leading coalition forces to secure the country.

Baghdad

As of June 2006

Baghdad

As of June 2007

☐ Iraqis in the Lead
69 Battalions

☐ Iraqis in the Lead
95 Battalions

Taken from: Department of Defense, June 2007.
www.defenselink.mil/home/dodupdate/iraq-update/Handovers/index.html.

throes." I repeatedly criticized the previous search-and-destroy strategy and argued for a counterinsurgency approach: separating the reconcilable population from the irreconcilable and creating enough security to facilitate the political and economic solutions that are the only way to defeat insurgents. This is exactly the course that Petraeus and the brave men and women of the American military are pursuing.

The new political-military strategy is beginning to show results. But most Americans are not aware because much of the media are not reporting it or devote far more attention to car bombs and mortar attacks that reveal little about the strategic direction of the war. I am not saying that bad news should not be reported or that horrific terrorist attacks are not newsworthy. But news coverage should also include evidence of progress. Whether Americans choose to support or oppose our efforts in Iraq, I hope they could make their decision based on as complete a picture of the situation in Iraq as is possible to report.

> ## Life Is Getting Better in Iraq
>
> For some Baghdadis, the security plan is starting to provide an opportunity for a few simple pleasures: a meal in a restaurant, a stroll inside heavily guarded parks and gardens, or a quick shopping trip despite the uncertain outlook. Overall, there has been a drop in sectarian-related murders and daily bombings due to the stepped up presence of U.S. and Iraqi forces on the streets.
>
> Sam Dagher, "Is Baghdad Safer? Yes and No," *Christian Science Monitor*, April 13, 2007. http://www.csmonitor.com/2007/0413/p01s04-woiq.html.

Examples of Success

A few examples:

- Sunni sheikhs in Anbar are now fighting al-Qaeda. Prime Minister Nouri al-Maliki visited Anbar's capital, Ramadi, to meet with Sunni tribal leaders. The newly proposed de-Baathification legislation grew out of that meeting. Police recruitment in Ramadi has increased dramatically over the past four months.
- More than 50 joint U.S.-Iraqi stations have been established in Baghdad. Regular patrols establish connections with the surrounding neighborhood, resulting in a significant increase in security and actionable intelligence.
- Extremist Shiite militia leader Moqtada al-Sadr is in hiding, his followers are not contesting American forces,

sectarian violence has dropped in Baghdad and we are working with the Shiite mayor of Sadr City.

- Iraqi army and police forces are increasingly fighting on their own and with American forces, and their size and capability are growing. Iraqi army and police casualties have increased because they are fighting more.

Finally, Iraq Is on the Right Track

Despite these welcome developments, we should have no illusions. This progress is not determinative. It is simply encouraging. We have a long, tough road ahead in Iraq. But for the first time since 2003, we have the right strategy. In Petraeus, we have a military professional who literally wrote the book on fighting this kind of war. And we will have the right mix and number of forces.

There is no guarantee that we will succeed, but we must try. As every sensible observer has concluded, the

The reopening of central Baghdad's Abu Nuwas street to traffic on November 24, 2007, was cause for celebration among the Iraqi people.

consequences of failure in Iraq are so grave and so threatening for the region, and to the security of the United States, that to refuse to give Petraeus's plan a chance to succeed would constitute a tragic failure of American resolve. . . . This is not a moment for partisan gamesmanship or for one-sided reporting. The stakes are just too high.

Analyze the essay:

1. McCain argues that good news about Iraq is underreported by the American news media. He does not, however, offer an explanation for why the media would do this. What do you think? Do the U.S. media focus more on bad news coming out of Iraq than good? If so, why would they do this? Or, do you not agree that good news is underreported? Explain your position.

2. John McCain is a politician who has visited Iraq many times. In what way does knowing his background influence the weight you give his argument? Do you think his status as a politician makes his perspective of on-the-ground Iraqi realities more or less credible? Explain your reasoning.

The Situation in Iraq Is Worsening

International Committee of the Red Cross

The International Committee of the Red Cross (ICRC) is a private humanitarian institution based in Geneva, Switzerland. The ICRC is charged with protecting and providing aid to the victims of international armed conflicts, including the wounded, prisoners, refugees, civilians, and other noncombatants. In the following viewpoint, writers for the ICRC paint a dire picture of the situation in Iraq. The authors claim the daily lives of Iraqis are steadily worsening due to rampant chaos in the country. Murders, kidnappings, and bombings have become so commonplace that many Iraqis are afraid to leave their homes. Violence and war have destroyed the country's infrastructure, resulting in power shortages, fuel shortages, and a lack of clean water. Medical care is widely unavailable, as medical facilities lack adequate supplies and many doctors have been forced to leave the country. For these reasons the ICRC concludes the situation in Iraq is worsening and implores politicians and humanitarian organizations to intervene.

Consider the following questions:

1. According to the ICRC, what public health risks do the Iraqi people face?
2. How many families have been displaced since February 2006, as reported by the ICRC?
3. How have road blocks and checkpoints impeded access to medical care, according to the authors?

International Committee of the Red Cross (www.icrc.org), "Civilians Without Protection: The Ever-Worsening Humanitarian Crisis in Iraq," April 11, 2007. Reproduced by permission.

The humanitarian situation is steadily worsening and it is affecting, directly or indirectly, all Iraqis.

Protecting Iraq's civilian population must be a priority, and the ICRC [International Committee of the Red Cross] urgently calls for better respect for international humanitarian law. It appeals to all those with military or political influence on the ground to act now to ensure that the lives of ordinary Iraqis are spared and protected. This is an obligation under international humanitarian law for both States and non-State actors.

The ICRC aims to ensure that Iraqis receive the aid they need most. It cooperates closely with the Iraqi Red Crescent [an Iraqi aid organization]. However, humanitarian aid is clearly not enough when it comes to addressing the immense needs of Iraqis in the present disastrous security situation.

The International Committee of the Red Cross (ICRC) has worked to help Iraqi civilians battle daily threats of kidnappings, bombings, and murders.

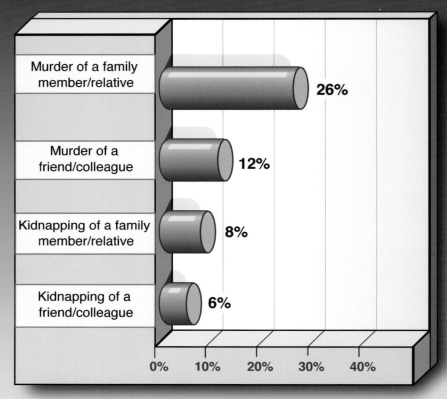

Iraqis Have Endured Violence and Murder

A 2007 poll found that more than half of all Iraqis (52 percent) had experienced the murder or kidnapping of someone close to them.

Murder of a family member/relative	26%
Murder of a friend/colleague	12%
Kidnapping of a family member/relative	8%
Kidnapping of a friend/colleague	6%

0% 10% 20% 30% 40%

Taken from: British Ministry of Defense, August 2005.

Shootings, Bombings, Abductions, and Murders

The conflict in Iraq is inflicting immense suffering on the entire population. Civilians bear the brunt of the relentless violence and the extremely poor security conditions that are disrupting the lives and livelihoods of millions. Every day, dozens of people are killed and many more wounded. The plight of Iraqi civilians is a daily reminder of the fact that there has long been a failure to respect their lives and dignity.

Shootings, bombings, abductions, murders, military operations and other forms of violence are forcing thousands of people to flee their homes and seek safety elsewhere in Iraq or in neighbouring countries. The hundreds of thousands of displaced people scattered across Iraq find it particularly difficult to cope with the ongoing crisis, as do the families who generously agree to host them.

Health-care facilities are stretched to the limit as they struggle to cope with mass casualties day-in, day-out. Many sick and injured people do not go to hospital because it's too dangerous, and the patients and medical staff in those facilities are frequently threatened or targeted.

Unemployment, Poverty, and Hunger on the Rise

Food shortages have been reported in several areas. According to the Iraqi Red Crescent, malnutrition has increased over the past year. The vastly inadequate water, sewage and electricity infrastructure is presenting a risk to public health. Unemployment and poverty levels are rising and many families continue to rely on government food distributions to cover their immediate needs. According to government sources, an estimated one third of the population lives in poverty, while over five percent live in extreme poverty.

A Crumbling Infrastructure

Much of Iraq's vital infrastructure is in a poor state of repair owing to lack of maintenance and because security constraints have impeded repair work on electrical power grids, water and sanitation systems, medical facilities and other essential facilities.

"We're Scared. But What Can We Do?"

I've been in the shop since morning. Not surprisingly, there's no one here yet, no customers. People are generally more afraid in the morning. Eventually they venture out. It is normal for us to see police cars and gunmen and the Americans all over the place, without knowing what on earth is going on. We just see them there, blocking roads, clashing with someone, firing at each other. Every day. It's become routine. We're afraid of any car on the streets. How can you know if it's rigged or not? You can't. We just pray and then leave home for work. We're sitting around. We're not feeling secure at all. We're scared. But what can we do?

Hairdresser and Baghdad resident Um Mustafa, quoted in "Iraqis' daily lives," BBC.com, April 7, 2006. http://news.bbc.co.uk/2/hi/middle_east/4881164.stm.

Power shortages are growing worse throughout the country, including northern areas, owing largely to the failure to carry out maintenance and to increase generation capacity. Fuel shortages affecting power stations and acts of sabotage are further aggravating the crisis. As a result, water-treatment plants, primary health-care centres and hospitals rely mainly on back-up generators, which often break down owing to excess usage or fall victim to the chronic fuel shortages. . . .

In some regions, particularly Baghdad and area, families are often too afraid to leave their homes to go to work or to shop and too afraid to send their children to school because of random violence and the threat of kidnapping for ransom.

Voices from the Conflict

"Once I was called to an explosion site. There I saw a four-year-old boy sitting beside his mother's body, which had been decapitated by the explosion. He was talking to her, asking her what had happened. He had been taken out shopping by his mom."

—Saad, a young humanitarian worker from Baghdad

"Some time ago, there was a shooting near Abu Hanifa Mosque between the police and an armed group. A young man passing by was hit by stray bullets and lay badly wounded and crying out for help. Because of the gunfire, nobody could get close to him to drag him out. He bled to death right in front of us."

—Raad, a shopkeeper in the Adhamia area of Baghdad

"I was accosted by gunmen who gave me two hours to leave my home, together with my wife and three children. They told me not to take any of my belongings, not even my children's clothes."

—Saad, an engineer from the Hurriya area of Baghdad

"You're lucky if you get a warning to leave your home. If you do, it means at least you have a chance to survive. You must be ready to flee your place any moment."

—An ICRC employee in Baghdad

Thousands Have Been Turned into Refugees

Since the bombing of the sacred Shiite shrine of Samarra in February 2006 and the subsequent increase in violence, the problem of displacement in Iraq has become particularly acute. Thousands of Iraqis continue to be forced out of their homes owing to military operations, general poor security and the destruction of houses. And the outlook is bleak, particularly in Baghdad and other areas with mixed communities, where the situation is likely to worsen.

Most displaced people have taken refuge with host families, who often struggle to cope with the additional burden on their limited resources. Some have found refuge in camps, public buildings and abandoned military barracks. Where displaced people decide to seek refuge often depends on the presence of relatives or friends and, because of the prevailing sectarian violence, on the religious or ethnic make-up of the host community.

The Iraqi Red Crescent estimates that approximately 106,000 families have been displaced inside the country since February 2006. It estimates that two thirds of the displaced are women and children, often living in female-headed households.

Families Are Barely Surviving

Frequently, both the displaced families and the communities hosting them are badly in need of shelter materials, access to clean water, adequate sanitation, food and other essentials.

The displacement of hundreds of thousands of people places an additional burden on Iraq's basic infrastructure, which is barely sufficient to serve the resident population.

Humanitarian aid is needed by a wide range of particularly vulnerable civilians, including elderly and disabled people and female-headed households.

The Medical Crisis

Medical professionals are fleeing the country in large numbers following the murder or abduction of colleagues. Hospitals and other key services are desperately short of

Volunteer workers tend to an Iraqi child after he fell victim to a terrorist attack. The number of terrorist attacks has increased since the start of the war.

qualified staff. According to the Iraqi Ministry of Health, more than half the doctors have left the country.

The mass influx of casualties to hospitals following the daily attacks against civilians and other violent incidents is putting the health-care system under tremendous additional strain. Staff and resources are often stretched to the limit.

The failure to observe the special status of medical staff and facilities is a major concern. A hospital director in Baghdad told the ICRC that poor security condi-

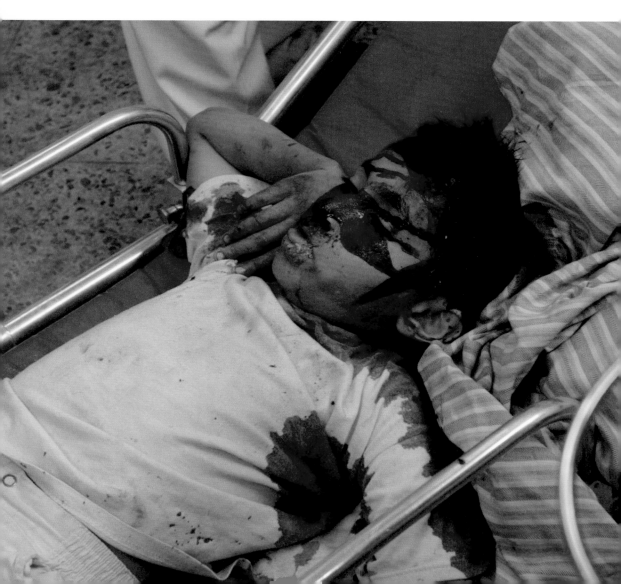

tions were preventing staff from providing medical services. And there have been frequent reports of armed men storming hospitals and forcing doctors to give their companions priority treatment at the expense of others in more urgent need.

Road-blocks and check-points sometimes prevent doctors and patients from reaching health-care centres in time. The lack of security also hampers the distribution of medical supplies in many parts of Iraq.

Dirty and Scarce—the Water Crisis

Both the quantity and quality of drinking water in Iraq remain insufficient despite limited improvements in some areas, mainly in the south. Water is often contaminated owing to the poor repair of sewage and water-supply networks and the discharge of untreated sewage into rivers, which are the main source of drinking water. Electricity and fuel shortages and the poor maintenance of infrastructure mean that there is no regular and reliable supply of clean water and that sewage is often not properly disposed of. Besides carrying out maintenance and repair work to ensure emergency water supplies, the ICRC is also trucking drinking water daily to displaced and other particularly vulnerable people. It also distributes water in sealed plastic bags.

Torn Apart—the Fate of Separated Families

The conflict has torn apart many families, with relatives being detained or fleeing their homes to seek safety elsewhere in Iraq or outside the country. Dispersed members of families often need help to locate loved ones and restore contact. Some have been without news of their loved ones for many years.

Tens of thousands of people are currently being detained by the Iraqi authorities and the multinational forces in Iraq. Many families remain without news of relatives who went missing during past conflicts or the current hostilities.

Visiting people detained in connection with the armed conflict in Iraq remains a humanitarian priority for the ICRC. Persons held by the multinational forces or the Kurdish regional government are regularly visited to assess their conditions of detention and treatment.

Analyze the essay:

1. This essay included first-person testimonials from Iraqi people describing their everyday realities. How did these help persuade you of the authors' viewpoint? In what way do such testimonials differ from other kinds of quotes?

2. The ICRC is a humanitarian organization that works with Iraqis in all parts of the country. Does knowing the organization's mission and purpose influence the weight you give its argument? Why or why not?

3. In the previous essay John McCain argues that the situation in Iraq is improving. In this essay the authors argue the situation is worsening. After reading both essays, with which viewpoint do you agree? What pieces of evidence helped you come to your conclusion? Explain your answer, citing evidence from the text.

The United States Must Leave Iraq Immediately

Jonathan P. Baird

The United States must leave Iraq as soon as possible, Jonathan P. Baird argues in the following essay. He explains that the war has been a disaster from the start, and Iraq is stuck in a seemingly endless cycle of murder and violence. Baird says it is not right that millions of dollars and thousands of lives have been wasted trying to fix a country that is beyond repair. Furthermore, argues Baird, it is not the job of U.S. soldiers to oversee a civil war, which he says is occurring in Iraq. Therefore, Baird concludes the United States should withdraw its troops immediately before it wastes even more money and ruins more lives.

Baird is an attorney who lives in New Hampshire.

Consider the following questions:

1. Baird says that the U.S. invasion of Iraq opened a Pandora's box. What does he mean by this?
2. As reported by the author, how much has the government spent on the war in Iraq thus far?
3. What similarities does Baird see between the Iraq War and the Vietnam War?

It is time for the United States to withdraw from Iraq. Not in five years or three years—withdrawal should start now and troops should be brought home within a year. The human and economic cost have proven to be too high.

Jonathan P. Baird, "Why We Must Leave Iraq," *New Hampshire Business Review*, vol. 29, January 5, 2007, p. 20. Copyright © 2007 Jonathan P. Baird. Reproduced by permission.

Cars carry dead bodies through an Iraqi city. Daily funeral processions like this one indicate that murder and violence are on the rise.

Repeating the Mistakes of Vietnam

The relevant parallel is our failure to leave Vietnam in 1968 when the country turned against that war. Instead of a real end, the war needlessly dragged on until 1975, adding thousands to the death and disability toll.

We must avoid another prolonged withdrawal that goes on for years and is, in fact, a cover for further occupation of Iraq. In spite of the election results that have been widely interpreted as a repudiation of the war, there is no visible withdrawal plan currently under public discussion in the government.

The Iraq War Has Been a Catastrophe

While it is no doubt presumptuous for a private citizen outside any elite to offer an opinion, candor requires a reckoning with the Iraq invasion and occupation. Whatever its multiple flawed and ever-changing justifications, the war must be recognized as a hell-catastrophe of almost unimaginable magnitude.

When we invaded Iraq, we opened Pandora's Box. Little understanding the society we arrogantly sought to remake, the result is a growing mountain of Iraqi and American corpses. Abductions, executions, car bombs, suicide bombers, IEDs, torture—Iraq is locked into endless cycles of murder and retaliation.

Our recent preoccupation with whether this is a civil war or a widening, vicious, sectarian conflict is a semantic distinction without consequence. Either way, revenge killings and ethnic cleansing are the order of the day. Neither the Iraqi government nor our troops have been able to stem the massacres.

Attacks in Iraq Have Increased Dramatically

The insurgency in Iraq has continued to launch attacks on U.S., coalition, and Iraqi forces since the invasion of Iraq in 2003. Thousands of attacks are launched every month, resulting in ongoing violence and instability in the country.

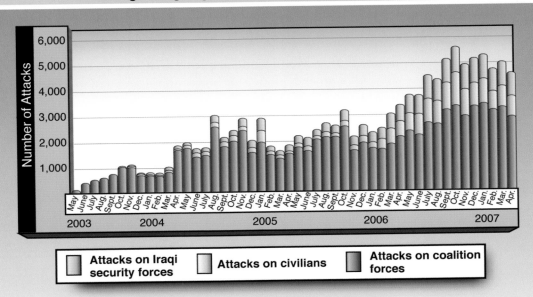

Taken from: Brookings Institution, *Iraq Index Tracking Variables of Reconstruction & Security in Post-Saddam Iraq*, August 6, 2007. www.brookings.edu/iraqindex.

Throwing Money at the Iraq Problem

Meanwhile, we are recklessly and pointlessly wasting the treasury of the United States on a monumental folly. According to costofwar.com, we have spent over $350 billion on the war. We add $8 billion a month on military spending in Iraq. The Pentagon has now asked for a supplemental appropriation of $160 billion for fiscal year 2007 for Iraq and Afghanistan.

Talk about throwing money at problems. Where is any party of fiscal responsibility? Congress has failed its oversight function. Billions of dollars spent in Iraq are unaccounted for. We desperately need congressional investigations into corruption and war profiteering. The principle of accountability must be restored.

To Improve Iraq, the United States Must Leave

The US occupation of Iraq is the cause of, not the solution to, the violence and the mounting deaths that followed the [2003] invasion. . . . The Bush Administration uses the fighting as justification for the continued presence of foreign military forces. Yet it is precisely the presence of foreign military forces that is a major cause of the instability. Ending the U.S. occupation by bringing the troops home now is a first step toward ending Iraq's nightmare.

Erik Leaver, "Top 10 Reasons for the US to Get Out of Iraq," *Nation*, October 11, 2004. http://www.the nation.com/doc/20041011/leaver.

U.S. Soldiers Deserve Better

The lives of our soldiers are too valuable to be wasted in a war that has lost any compelling rationale. Can anyone give a coherent argument for why our soldiers should oversee a slaughter between an array of incomprehensible warring Iraqi factions?

We have been told that we must stay to prevent a bloodbath and a further unraveling of the country. The bad news is that the bloodbath has already happened.

In this context, President Bush's words about victory ring utterly hollow. They mask a too cavalier attitude toward the blood already spilled, not to mention a disconnect from the reality-based community.

It is likely the war-spinners will tell us that more sophisticated counterinsurgency, greater force and improved tactics will work. They will paint scenarios of greater horror if we leave. Based on their track record, we would be fools to heed their advice.

America Should Leave Before Things Get Worse

In truth, no one knows where this war is heading. I believe it would be better to cut our losses than compound the mayhem. A diplomatic approach involving the United Nations and all the nations in the region would be far superior to the Bush administration's unilateral militarism.

Future historians will have to decide the reasons for this war. Oil, control of the region, neoconservative and evangelical fantasy all come to mind. If history offers a

U.S. troops struggle daily in Iraq with ongoing attacks, which cost millions of dollars and many lives.

way of learning, we will hopefully learn humility. Having lived through Vietnam, I never thought we would repeat that quagmire so soon. I was wrong.

Enough with the vainglorious pursuit of empire like some 19th century colonialist power. Enough with pouring money down a bottomless rat hole unrelated to the needs of American citizens. Priorities must shift back to the neglected needs of our own citizens.

Analyze the essay:
1. Baird likens the United States to a nineteenth-century colonialist power. Given what you know on this topic, do you think this is an appropriate comparison? Why or why not? Explain your reasoning.
2. Baird does not use any quotations to support his argument. If you could go back and insert quotations in his essay, where you put them? What types of voices would you include?

The United States Cannot Yet Leave Iraq

Economist

In the following essay editors at the London-based news magazine the *Economist* explain why they believe the United States must not yet withdraw its troops from Iraq. Withdrawing U.S. troops prematurely would undo the progress that has been made since the 2003 invasion of that country, they argue. Iraq has held successful elections and stabilized sections of its country—but has only been able to do so because of the presence of U.S. troops. If troops are withdrawn, Iraq will surely fall into chaos, argue the authors. Should this happen, militant Islamists and terrorists around the world will be emboldened in their cause. Therefore, for both the future of Iraq and the success of America in the war on terror, the United States must not leave Iraq until it is better stabilized.

Consider the following questions:

1. Who is John Murtha? What do the authors think of his position on troop withdrawal from Iraq?
2. What should all reasonable people agree on regarding America's position in Iraq, according to the authors?
3. How many of Iraq's provinces have insurgents been reduced to, as reported by the authors?

Wars waged abroad are often lost at home; and that may be starting to happen with Iraq. Calls for American troops to withdraw are familiar in the Arab world and Europe, but in the United States itself such talk

The presence of U.S. troops has helped stabilize relationships among the Iraqi people. For this reason, it is argued their presence is critical to maintaining peace.

has remained on the fringes of political debate. Now, with surprising suddenness, it has landed at the centre of American politics.

Those Who Want America to Leave Iraq

On November 17th [2005] John Murtha, a hawkish Democratic congressman, suggested pulling the troops out of Iraq in six months, prompting an unseemly spat between the former marine colonel and the White House. Moves to set a timetable have been voted down, but the Republican-controlled Senate has voted 79–19 for 2006 to be "a period of significant transition to full Iraq sovereignty" and the Pentagon is mumbling about troop reductions. Meanwhile, some hundred Iraqi leaders at a reconciliation conference in Cairo backed by the Arab League talked about setting a timetable for withdrawal.

There is some politicking in this. In Cairo, the Shias and Kurds, who dominate Iraq's new order, were offering an olive branch to the sullen Sunnis, who used to run the show under [former Iraqi dictator] Saddam Hussein. In America, Republicans are looking nervously at the 2006 elections. Democrats sense that George Bush is vulnerable—and that Iraq presents the best way to hurt him now that most Americans regret invading the country. Yet there is plainly principle too: Mr Murtha and millions of others maintain that America is doing more harm than good in Iraq, and that the troops should therefore come home.

Withdrawing from Iraq Would Be Disastrous

This newspaper [the *Economist*] strongly disagrees. In our opinion it would be disastrous for America to retreat hastily from Iraq. Yet it is also well past time for George Bush to spell out to the American people much more clearly and honestly than he has hitherto done why their sons and daughters fighting in Iraq should remain in harm's way.

Every reasonable person should be able to agree on two things about America's presence in Iraq. First, if the Iraqi government formally asks the troops to leave, they should do so. Second, the argument about whether America should quit Iraq is not the same as the one about whether it should have gone there in the first place. It must be about the future.

There Is No Doubt Things Are Difficult in Iraq

That said, the catalogue of failures thus far does raise serious questions about the administration's ability to make Iraq work—ever. Mr Bush's team mis-sold the war, neglected post-invasion planning, has never committed enough troops to the task and has taken a cavalier attitude to human rights. Abu Ghraib, a place of unspeakable suffering under Mr Hussein, will go into the history books as a symbol of American shame.[1] The awful irony is that the specious link which the administration claimed existed between Iraq and al-Qaeda in order to justify going to war now exists.

> ## War Gets Worse Before It Gets Better
>
> We forget that once war breaks out, things usually get far worse before they get better. We should remember that 1943, after we had entered World War II, was a far bloodier year than 1938, when the world left [Adolf] Hitler alone. Similarly, 2005 may have brought more open violence in Iraq than was visible during Saddam's less publicized killings of 2002. So it is when extremists are confronted rather than appeased.
>
> Victor Davis Hanson, "Why We Must Stay in Iraq," *Washington Post*, September 4, 2005.

1. The Iraqi prison Abu Ghraib was where American soldiers abused Iraqi prisoners in 2003.

U.S. troops have helped Iraqis make considerable progress, such as the establishment of elections, and giving women the right to vote.

Two-and-a-half years after Mr Bush stood beneath a banner proclaiming "Mission Accomplished", the insurgency is as strong as ever. More than 2,000 Americans, some 3,600 Iraqi troops, perhaps 30,000 Iraqi civilians and an unknown number of Iraqi insurgents have lost their lives, and conditions of life for the "liberated" remain woeful. All this makes Mr Bush's refusal to sack the people responsible for this mess, especially his defence secretary, Donald Rumsfeld,[2] alarming.

But disappointment, even on this scale, does not justify a precipitate withdrawal. There are strong positive and negative reasons for America to see through what it started. . . .

Progress Is Being Made

Iraq is not Vietnam. Most Iraqis share America's aims: the Shia Arabs and Kurds make up some 80% of the population, while the insurgents operate mainly in four of Iraq's 18 provinces. After boycotting the first general election in January [2005], more Sunni Arabs are taking part in peaceful politics. Many voted in last month's [October

2. Donald Rumsfeld resigned as secretary of defense in 2006.

2005] referendum that endorsed a new constitution; more should be drawn into next month's [December 2005] election, enabling a more representative government to emerge. That will not stop the insurgency, but may lessen its intensity. It seems, too, that the Arab world may be turning against the more extreme part of the insurgency—the jihadists led by al-Qaeda's leader in Iraq, Abu Musab al-Zarqawi, who blow up mosques around Baghdad and Palestinian wedding parties in Jordan. . . . Though few Arabs publicly admit it, Mr Bush's efforts to spread democracy in the region are starting to bear fruit.

More Troops Are Needed, Not Less

So America does have something to defend in Iraq. Which, for Mr Bush's critics, leads into the most tempting part of Mr Murtha's argument: that American troops are now a barrier to further progress; that if they left, Mr Zarqawi would lose the one thing that unites the Sunnis and jihadists; and that, in consequence, Iraqis would have to look after their own security. This has a seductive logic,

© 2007 Eric Allie, and Politicalcartoons.com.

but flies in the face of the evidence. Most of the insurgents' victims are Iraqis, not American soldiers. There are still too few American troops, not too many. And the Iraqi forces that America is training are not yet ready to stand on their own feet. By all means, hand over more duties to them, letting American and other coalition troops withdraw from the cities where they are most conspicuous and offensive to patriotic Iraqis. Over time, American numbers should fall. But that should happen because the Iraqis are getting stronger, not because the Americans are feeling weaker. Nor should a fixed timetable be set, for that would embolden the insurgents.

"The Consequences of Leaving Would Be Too Awful"

The cost to America of staying in Iraq may be high, but the cost of retreat would be higher. By fleeing, America would not buy itself peace. Mr Zarqawi and his fellow fanatics have promised to hound America around the globe. Driving America out of Iraq would grant militant Islam a huge victory. Arabs who want to modernise their region would know that they could not count on America to stand by its friends.

If such reasoning sounds negative—America must stay because the consequences of leaving would be too awful—treat that as a sad reflection of how Mr Bush's vision for the Middle East has soured. The road ahead looks bloody and costly. But this is not the time to retreat.

Analyze the essay:

1. The authors warn that pulling out of Iraq now could have disastrous consequences for the United States in Iraq and elsewhere in the world. How do you think Jonathan P. Baird, author of the previous essay, would respond to his claim?
2. Both authors agree that the war in Iraq has not gone very well. But they have different opinions on whether troops should stay or go. How do you account for this?

Section Two:
Model Essays
and Writing
Exercises

The Five-Paragraph Essay

A n *essay* is a short piece of writing that discusses or analyzes one topic. The five-paragraph essay is a form commonly used in school assignments and tests. Every five-paragraph essay begins with an *introduction,* ends with a *conclusion,* and features three *supporting paragraphs* in the middle.

The Thesis Statement. The introduction includes the essay's thesis statement. The thesis statement presents the argument or point the author is trying to make about the topic. The essays in this book all have different thesis statements because they are making different arguments about the war in Iraq.

The thesis statement should clearly tell the reader what the essay will be about. A focused thesis statement helps determine what will be in the essay; the subsequent paragraphs are spent developing and supporting its argument.

The Introduction. In addition to presenting the thesis statement, a well-written introductory paragraph captures the attention of the reader and explains why the topic being explored is important. It may provide the reader with background information on the subject matter or feature an anecdote that illustrates a point relevant to the topic. It could also present startling information that clarifies the point of the essay or put forth a contradictory position that the essay will refute. Further techniques for writing an introduction are found later in this section.

The Supporting Paragraphs. The introduction is followed by three (or more) supporting paragraphs. These are the main body of the essay. Each paragraph presents and develops a *subtopic* that supports the essay's thesis statement. Each subtopic is then supported with its own facts, details, and examples. The writer can use various kinds of supporting material and details to back up the topic of each supporting paragraph. These may include statistics, quotations from people with special knowledge or expertise, historic facts, and anecdotes. A rule of writing is that specific and concrete examples are more convincing than vague, general, or unsupported assertions.

The Conclusion. The conclusion is the paragraph that closes the essay. Its function is to summarize or reiterate the main idea of the essay. It may recall an idea from the introduction or briefly examine the larger implications of the thesis. Because the conclusion is also the last chance a writer has to make an impression on the reader, it is important that it not simply repeat what has been presented elsewhere in the essay, but close it in a clear, final, and memorable way.

Although the order of the essay's component paragraphs is important, they do not have to be written in that order. Some writers like to decide on a thesis and write the introduction paragraph first. Other writers like to focus first on the body of the essay and write the introduction and conclusion later.

Pitfalls to Avoid

When writing essays about controversial issues such as the Iraq War, it is important to remember that disputes over the material are common precisely because there are many different perspectives. Remember to state your arguments in careful and measured terms. Evaluate your topic fairly—avoid overstating negative qualities of one perspective or understating positive qualities of another. Use examples, facts, and details to support any assertions you make.

The Persuasive Essay

There are many types of essays, but in general, they are usually short compositions in which the writer expresses and discusses an opinion about something. In the persuasive essay the writer tries to persuade (convince) the reader to do something or to agree with the writer's opinion about something. Examples of persuasive writing are easy to find. Advertising is one common example. Through commercial and print ads, companies try to convince the public to buy their products for specific reasons. Much everyday writing is persuasive, too. Letters to the editor, posts from sports fans on team Web sites, even handwritten notes urging a friend to listen to a new CD—all are examples of persuasive writing.

The Tools of Persuasion

The writer of the persuasive essay uses various tools to persuade the reader. Here are some of them:

Facts and Statistics. A fact is a statement that no one, typically, would disagree with. It can be verified by information in reputable resources, such as encyclopedias, almanacs, government Web sites, or reference books about the topic of the fact.

Examples of Facts and Statistics

Christmas is celebrated on December 25.

Albany is the capital of New York.

The average American eats 159 fast food meals each year.

According to the American Psychological Association, 73 percent of Americans list money as the number one factor that stresses them out.

It is important to note that facts and statistics can be *misstated* (written down or quoted incorrectly), *misinterpreted* (not understood correctly by the user), or *misused* (not used fairly). But, if a writer uses facts and statistics properly, they can add authority to the writer's essay.

Opinions. An opinion is what a person thinks about something. It can be contested or argued with. However, opinions of people who are experts on the topic or who have personal experience are often very convincing. Many persuasive essays are written to convince the reader that the writer's opinion is worth believing and acting on.

Testimonials. A testimonial is a statement given by a person who is thought to be an expert or who has another trait people admire, such as being a celebrity. The statement is given by someone who has firsthand knowledge about a subject. Television commercials frequently use testimonials to convince watchers to buy the products they are advertising.

Examples and Anecdotes. An example is something that is representative of a group or type (*blue* is an example of the group *color*). Examples are used to help define, describe, or illustrate something to make it more understandable. Anecdotes are extended examples. They are little stories with a beginning, middle, and end. They can be used just like examples to explain something or to show something about a topic.

Appeals to Reason. One way to convince readers that an opinion or action is right is to appeal to reason or logic. This often involves the idea that if some ideas are true, another must also be true. Here is an example of one type of appeal to reason:

- Turtle Homes Rescue is an organization that rescues many turtles every year.
- Turtle Homes Rescue needs money to keep operating. Therefore, if you love animals, you should contribute money to Turtle Homes Rescue.

Appeals to Emotion. Another way to persuade readers to believe or do something is to appeal to their emotions— love, fear, pity, loyalty, and anger are some of the emotions to which writers appeal. A writer who wants to persuade the reader that Americans should be drafted into the military might appeal to the reader's sense of loyalty: "Every American must equally share the responsibility of protecting this nation—we cannot let only the bravest and most responsible members of society carry this heavy burden that benefits us all."

Ridicule and Name-calling. Ridicule and name-calling are not good techniques to use in a persuasive essay. Instead of exploring the strengths of the topic, the writer who uses these relies on making those who oppose the main idea look foolish, evil, or stupid. In most cases, the writer who does this weakens the argument.

Bandwagon. The writer who uses the bandwagon technique uses the idea that "everybody thinks this or is doing this; therefore it is valid." The bandwagon method is not a very authoritative way to convince your reader of your point.

Words and Phrases Common to Persuasive Essays

accordingly	it seems clear that
because	it stands to reason
consequently	it then follows that
clearly	obviously
for this reason	since
this is why	subsequently
indeed	therefore
it is necessary to	thus
it makes sense to	we must

We Can't Leave Yet

Essay
One

Editor's Notes The first model essay argues that U.S. troops should not yet be pulled from Iraq. The author explains why she believes withdrawing troops prematurely from the Iraq conflict would be disastrous for both Iraqis and Americans. The essay is structured as a five-paragraph essay in which each paragraph contributes a supporting piece of evidence to develop the argument.

The notes in the margin point out key features of the essay and will help you understand how the essay is organized. Also note that all sources are cited using Modern Language Association (MLA) style.* For more information on how to cite your sources, see Appendix C. In addition, consider the following:

1. How does the introduction engage the reader's attention?
2. What persuasive techniques are used in the essay?
3. What purpose do the essay's quotes serve?
4. Does the essay convince you of its point?

> Refers to thesis and topic sentences

> Refers to supporting details

Paragraph 1

In March 2007 a CNN poll found that for the first time since the 2003 invasion, the majority of Americans—54 percent—believe that the United States is unable to win the Iraq War. The war has always been a divisive and contentious issue, but not until 2007 did more Americans think it was unwinnable than not. Because of this mental shift, and along with much-reported violence and chaos in Iraq, it has been suggested that the United States withdraw its forces from Iraq immediately, regardless of whether the country is stabilized or not.

This statistic was taken from Appendix A in this book. Look for other pieces of information that can be used to support essays.

---

* In applying MLA style guidlines in this book, the following simplifications have been made: Parenthetical text citations are confined to direct quotations only; electronic source documentation in the Works Cited list omits date of access, page ranges, and some detailed facts of publication.

However, withdrawing troops prematurely is a terrible idea that could ruin America's credibility and increase terrorism around the globe, among other disasters.

Paragraph 2

Leaving too soon would put a cap on Iraq's potential as a free and democratic nation. While it may be difficult to imagine it as such a place today, Iraq does have the potential to be a flourishing, safe, free country such as its neighbors Israel and Turkey. Americans would do well to remember that *all* battlefields are messy, dangerous, and bloody before they become monuments in free countries. Indeed, war is one indication such freedom is on the horizon, not an indication that freedom is lost. As Professor Victor Davis Hanson has explained, "We forget that once war breaks out, things usually get far worse before they get better. We should remember that 1943, after we had entered World War II, was a far bloodier year than 1938, when the world left [Adolf] Hitler alone. Similarly, 2005 may have brought more open violence in Iraq than was visible during Saddam's less publicized killings of 2002. So it is when extremists are confronted rather than appeased." Hanson uses history to remind us that the violence in modern-day Iraq is part and parcel of its struggle to a brighter day, rather than the signaling of its opposite.

Paragraph 3

In addition, to abandon Iraq before it is stabilized is to help terrorism spread further around the globe. Although it is debatable how involved Iraq was in terrorism under Saddam Hussein before the war, one thing is certain now: It is a hotbed of terrorism today, and the absolute center of the global war on terror. As the editors of the political magazine the *Economist* have noted, "The awful irony is that the specious link which the administration claimed existed between Iraq and al-Qaeda in order to justify going to war now exists." Indeed, terrorists flock to Iraq from all over the world to fight in what they see as the battle between good and evil. Should America retreat, those terrorists will feel they have won. More importantly, they will head to other weak, unstable countries to wage similar attempts. America must squash these terrorists while they are concentrated in Iraq instead of allowing them to spread like a cancer to the far corners of the globe.

Paragraph 4

Finally, to withdraw troops from Iraq before the job is done is to waste all of the time, money, and human life that have gone into the effort thus far. And it is no small amount that has been invested: As of September 2007 the war has cost U.S. taxpayers more than $600 billion dollars. The lives of more than 3,750 soldiers have been lost, in addition to as many as 77,000 Iraqi civilians. If Americans care to honor the soldiers it sends to war and the Iraqi people it purports to want to help, it would do well to make sure those who have died did not do so in vain.

This is the topic sentence of paragraph 4. How does it support the essay's thesis?

What persuasive technique is the author using here? See Preface B in this section for information on persuasive techniques.

Paragraph 5

These are just three of the many good reasons why U.S. troops must not be withdrawn from Iraq before the time is right. The right time will be when Iraqi police have been adequately trained to control violence, when foreign terrorists currently active in the country have been sent packing, and when sectarian violence between different Iraqi ethnic groups has dwindled to a nonthreatening minimum. If America stands by Iraq through this critical juncture, there is reward for everyone involved. But if America leaves before the time is right, Iraq's chances for being a free, safe, and democratic state will disappear with the last U.S. Humvee.

Note the conclusion does not restate the points that have been made in the essay, but wraps up the author's presentation in a useful way.

Works Cited

Hanson, Victor Davis. "Why We Must Stay in Iraq." *Washington Post* 4 Sept. 2005.

"Why America Must Stay—America and Iraq." *Economist* 26 Nov. 2005.

Exercise 1A: Create an Outline from an Existing Essay

It often helps to create an outline of the five-paragraph essay before you write it. The outline can help you organize the information, arguments, and evidence you have gathered during your research.

For this exercise, create an outline that could have been used to write "We Can't Leave Yet." This "reverse engineering" exercise is meant to help familiarize you with how outlines can help classify and arrange information.

To do this you will need to
1. articulate the essay's thesis,
2. pinpoint important pieces of evidence,
3. flag quotes that support the essay's ideas, and
4. identify key points that support the argument.

Part of the outline has already been started to give you an idea of the assignment.

Outline

I. Paragraph 1:
Write the essay's thesis: U.S. troops should not yet be pulled from Iraq.

II. Paragraph 2 topic:

A. Iraq has the potential to be a flourishing, safe, free country such as its neighbors Israel and Turkey.
B. Victor Davis Hanson quote that supports the idea that wars get worse before they get better.

III. Paragraph 3 topic: If the United States abandons Iraq, terrorism will spread around the globe.

A.

B. Once unoccupied in Iraq, terrorists will head to other weak, unstable countries.

IV. Paragraph 4 topic:

A.

B.

V. Paragraph 5:

A. Write the essay's conclusion:

Exercise 1B: Create an Outline for Your Own Essay

The first model essay expresses a particular point of view about the Iraq War. For this exercise, your assignment is to find supporting ideas, choose specific and concrete details, create an outline, and ultimately write a five-paragraph essay making a different, or even opposing, point about the Iraq War. Your goal is to use persuasive techniques to convince your reader.

Part I: Write a thesis statement.

The following thesis statement would be appropriate for an opposing essay on why the United States should withdraw its troops from Iraq immediately:

The United States could continue to throw good life and money after bad in Iraq, or it could come to the better conclusion that this war is unable to be won and we will make more friends by ending it than continuing it.

Or see the sample paper topics suggested in Appendix D for more ideas.

Part II: Brainstorm pieces of supporting evidence.

Using information from some of the viewpoints in the previous section and from the information found in Section Three of this book, write down three arguments or pieces of evidence that support the thesis statement you selected. Then, for each of these three arguments, write down facts, examples, and details that support it. These could be

- statistical information;
- personal memories and anecdotes;
- quotes from experts, peers, or family members;
- observations of people's actions and behaviors;
- specific and concrete details.

Supporting pieces of evidence for the above sample thesis statement are found in this book and include:

- Quote from Jonathan P. Baird in Viewpoint Five: "We are recklessly and pointlessly wasting the treasury of the United States on a monumental folly."
- Chart accompanying Viewpoint Five showing the increase of insurgency attacks against U.S., coalition, and Iraqi troops. The increase of attacks corresponds to the length of time the United States has been in Iraq.
- August 2005 British Ministry of Defense poll cited in Appendix A showing that 82 percent of Iraqis are strongly opposed to the presence of coalition troops in their country.

Part III: Place the information from Part I in outline form.

Part IV: Write the arguments or supporting statements in paragraph form.

By now you have three arguments that support the paragraph's thesis statement, as well as supporting material. Use the outline to write out your three supporting arguments in paragraph form. Make sure each paragraph has a topic sentence that states the paragraph's thesis clearly and broadly. Then, add supporting sentences that express the facts, quotes, details, and examples that support the paragraph's argument. The paragraph may also have a concluding or summary sentence.

The Iraq War: Encouraging the Spread of WMDs

Essay Two

Editor's Notes The following model essay argues that the Iraq War has encouraged other nations to acquire weapons of mass destruction. The essay is structured as a five-paragraph essay in which each paragraph contributes a supporting piece of evidence to develop the argument. Three distinct ways in which the Iraq War has encouraged other nations to develop weapons of mass destruction are explored.

As you read this essay, take note of its components and how they are organized (the notes in the margins provide further explanation).

Paragraph 1

When the Iraq War was launched in 2003, it was ostensibly to prevent Saddam Hussein from using or selling to terrorists weapons of mass destruction he was believed to own. In this way, the war was believed necessary to prevent the spread of weapons of mass destruction. However, the Iraq War has achieved the opposite effect; it did not prevent the spread of weapons of mass destruction, and in fact encouraged nations who do not yet have weapons of mass destruction to acquire them.

This is the essay's thesis statement. It tells the reader what will be argued in the following paragraphs.

Paragraph 2

The Iraq War likely caused the leaders of rogue nations such as Iran to hasten, rather than abandon, their nuclear weapons programs. Iran has long been suspected of attempting to build weapons of mass destruction. The invasion of Iraq was intended to signal to Iranian leaders that if a nation pursues weapons of mass destruction in violation of international law, there are heavy consequences. But instead, Iranian leaders likely saw Iraq's *lack* of nuclear weapons as a critical weakness that allowed its regime to be overthrown by the United States. Indeed, the leaders of Iran probably learned that the best way to protect themselves against an

This is the topic sentence of paragraph 2. It tells what piece of the argument this paragraph will focus on.

invasion is to get weapons of mass destruction—and as soon as possible! As law professor Liaquat Ali Khan explains, "The war on Iraq demonstrates that a state without weapons of mass destruction is vulnerable to invasion and occupation. It would be perfectly logical to conclude that Iraq was attacked not because it had weapons of mass destruction but because it had none." In this way, the war in Iraq likely spurred certain nations to preserve their security by adding to their arsenal.

In what way does the quote support the argument being made in this paragraph?

Paragraph 3

The Iraq War also has shown rogue nations such as Iran and North Korea that there is no reward for cooperating with international weapons inspectors, who are one of the front lines of defense against the spread of weapons of mass destruction. Weapons inspectors are sent into countries to make sure governments are complying with international law and using their nuclear technology for peaceful, rather than militaristic, purposes. Iraq had complied repeatedly with international weapons inspectors but was attacked anyway. North Korea, on the other hand, which has repeatedly denied weapons inspectors, has not been attacked. Political science professor Stephen Zunes explains in more detail: "Iraq, which had given up its nuclear program over a decade earlier and subsequently allowed International Atomic Energy Agency [IAEA] inspectors back in the country to verify the absence of such a program, was invaded and occupied by the United States. By contrast, North Korea—which reneged on its agreement and has apparently resumed production of nuclear weapons—has not been invaded" (29). Zunes and others think that rogue nations such as Iran will come to the conclusion that the recipe for avoiding invasion by the United States is to deny weapons inspectors access and develop weapons of mass destruction fast enough to deter an invasion.

What is the topic sentence of paragraph 3?

The author has chosen to quote a political science professor, who is someone with high-level knowledge about the topic. Always quote sources that can credibly speak on your topic.

Paragraph 4

Indeed, anyone with half a brain can agree that the Iraq War has not helped prevent the spread of weapons of mass destruction because it has diverted authorities' attention away from more pressing WMD threats. In fact, it now appears clear that Saddam Hussein never even had any weapons of mass destruction—but while the United States wasted years determining that, another, more menacing threat has sprung up: the regime of North Korea. North Korea has long been suspected of pursuing a nuclear weapons program in violation of international law. Sure enough, on October 9, 2006, it proved the world correct by successfully testing its first nuclear bomb. North Korea is now believed to possess enough highly enriched uranium to make between six and ten small nuclear weapons. According to more than one hundred foreign policy experts polled in 2007, the Iraq War in part allowed this to occur. More than two-thirds of the experts agree that diverting attention from North Korea to Iraq was a critical mistake, arguing that Iraq is not the central front in the war on terrorism. In addition, the majority of experts say over the next five years it is more important to disarm North Korea than to secure and stabilize Iraq.

"Indeed," "In fact," "Sure enough," and "In addition" are all transitional phrases that keep the ideas flowing. See Preface B for a list of such words commonly found in persuasive essays.

Paragraph 5

These are just three of the ways in which the Iraq War failed to prevent the spread of weapons of mass destruction around the world. On the contrary, it inspired rogue, terrorist-connected nations such as Iran and North Korea to hurry up and develop such weapons in order to be strong enough so the United States would be deterred from attacking. In terms of making the world a safer place, the Iraq War has been unsuccessful. World leaders must learn from these mistakes and ensure the next few years are spent improving, rather than worsening, the problem of weapons of mass destruction in our world.

This sentence serves to wrap up what the essay has discussed. It does so without repeating every point that was made.

After reading the essay, are you convinced of the author's points? If so, what evidence swayed you? If not, why not?

Works Cited

Khan, Liaquat Ali. "On the Brink: Nuclear Non-Proliferation Treaty Poised to Fall Apart." *Counterpunch.org* 4 May 2005 < www.counterpunch.org/khan05042005.html > .

Zunes, Stephen. "The Iranian Nuclear Threat: Myth and Reality." *Tikkun* Jan–Feb 2007: 29.

Exercise 2A: Create an Outline from an Existing Essay

As you did for the first model essay in this section, create an outline that could have been used to write "The Iraq War: Encouraging the Spread of WMDs." Be sure to identify the essay's thesis statement, its supporting ideas, and key pieces of evidence that were used.

Exercise 2B: Identify Persuasive Techniques

Essayists use many techniques to persuade you to agree with their ideas or to do something they want you to do. Some of the most common techniques are described in Preface B of this section, "The Persuasive Essay." These tools are facts and statistics, opinions, testimonials, examples and anecdotes, appeals to reason, appeals to emotion, ridicule and name-calling, and bandwagon. Go back to the preface and review these tools. Remember that most of these tools can be used to enhance your essay, but some of them—particularly ridiculing, name-calling, and bandwagon—can detract from the essay's effectiveness. Nevertheless, you should be able to recognize them in the essays you read.

Some writers use one persuasive tool throughout their whole essay. For example, the essay may be one extended anecdote, or the writer may rely entirely on statistics. But most writers typically use a combination of persuasive tools. Model Essay Two, "The Iraq War: Encouraging the Spread of WMDs," does this.

Problem One
Read Model Essay Two again and see if you can find every persuasive tool used. Put that information in the following table. Part of the table is filled in for you.

Explanatory notes are underneath the table. (Note: You will not fill in every box. No paragraph contains all of the techniques.)

	Paragraph 1 Sentence #	Paragraph 2 Sentence #	Paragraph 3 Sentence #	Paragraph 4 Sentence #	Paragraph 5 Sentence #
Fact				8–10[a]	
Statistic				10–11[b]	
Opinion					5[c]
Testimonial					
Example					
Anecdote					
Appeal to Reason		5–8[d]			
Appeal to Emotion					
Ridicule					
Name-Calling					
Bandwagon					

Notes

a. That North Korea has enough uranium to make between six and ten nuclear weapons is a fact.
b. The opinion of two-thirds of foreign policy experts polled is a statistic.
c. That the Iraq War was unsuccessful is a matter of opinion.
d. The author appeals to the reader's sense of reason by arguing that Iranian leaders are going to see that Iraq's downfall was due to its lack of defense. They will thus want to avoid making the same mistake and seek to acquire nuclear weapons.

Now, look at the table you have produced. Which persuasive tools does this essay rely on most heavily? Which are not used at all?

Problem Two
Apply this exercise to the other model essays in this section, and the viewpoints in Section One, when you are finished reading them.

The Iraq War Has Created More Terrorists

Editor's Notes The final model essay argues that the Iraq War has worsened the global terrorist problem. Supported by facts, quotes, statistics and opinions, it tries to persuade the reader that the Iraq War has both created new terrorists and fueled the ambitions of already existing terrorists.

This essay differs from the previous model essays in that it is longer than five paragraphs. Sometimes five paragraphs are simply not enough to develop an idea adequately. Extending the length of an essay can allow the reader to explore a topic in more depth or present multiple pieces of evidence that together provide a complete picture of a topic. Longer essays can also help readers discover the complexity of a subject by examining a topic beyond its superficial exterior. Moreover, the ability to write a sustained research or position paper is a valuable skill you will need as you advance academically.

As you read, consider the questions posed in the margins. Continue to identity the thesis statement, supporting details, transitions, and quotations. Examine the introductory and concluding paragraphs to understand how they give shape to the essay. Finally, evaluate the essay's general structure and assess its overall effectiveness.

- Refers to thesis and topic sentences
- Refers to supporting details

Paragraph 1

What is the essay's thesis statement? How did you identify it?

In 2003 Iraq was believed to be a state sponsor of terror. Operating under the assumption that Iraq's leader, Saddam Hussein, was supporting terrorists, the United States invaded as a part of the goal of the war on terror to reduce terrorism. However, since the invasion, quite the opposite has happened. The war in Iraq that was ostensibly undertaken to reduce global terrorism and make all countries in the world safer, in fact, has done the opposite.

Paragraph 2

Iraq has seen an increase in domestic terrorism every year since the war began. In 2005, according to the National Counterterrorism Center's *Country Reports on Terrorism, 2005*, Iraq was the scene of so many attacks, it accounted for more than 30 percent of the worldwide terrorist attacks and 55 percent of the fatalities (approximately 8,300). Indeed, more than 3,500 attacks were perpetrated in Iraq in just that year. Most often, suicide, car, or other types of bombs were intended to cause chaos and disrupt the rebuilding efforts of the country—in these cases, terrorists hit police headquarters and government offices. Sometimes the attacks were intended to damage infrastructure, and thus targeted gas or oil pipelines, roads, transportation system, and educational institutions. Still other attacks were intended to cause social upheaval and pit Iraq's various ethnicities against each other; in these attacks, religious sites such as mosques and shrines were attacked.

> What is the topic sentence of paragraph 2? What pieces of evidence are used to show that it is true?

Paragraph 3

The year 2005 was a bad year for terrorism in Iraq, but things only got worse in 2006. In fact, between 2005 and 2006, terrorism in Iraq jumped more than 90 percent. According to the 2006 version of the National Counterterrorism Center's report, Iraq accounted for 45 percent of the more than 14,000 terrorist incidents worldwide and for 65 percent of deaths from terrorism worldwide (more than 13,000 deaths in Iraq alone). It is for this reason that one terrorist who goes by the name Abu Zabihullah has said, "Iraq is where the fierce encounters take place, where we recruit and dispatch fighters and where jihad's spirit thrives" (qtd. in Nordland 38).

> Where are these statistics taken from—authoritative sources? What points do they serve to support?

Paragraph 4

In addition to increasing terrorism in Iraq, the war in Iraq has also worsened the terrorist problem all around the globe. Indeed, since the March 2003 invasion, terrorism worldwide has increased by more than 5,000 percent. From this perspective it seems clear that the Iraq War is creating, rather than eradicating, terrorists. When asked

> Make a list of everyone quoted in this essay. What types of people have been quoted? What makes them qualified to speak on this topic?

his opinion on the Iraq War's impact on global terrorism, former national intelligence officer Paul Pillar says, "With particular reference to the impact of the Iraq war, the unfortunate answer is yes, we are creating them [terrorists] faster than we capture or kill them" (qtd. in "Rumsfeld Skeptical of Intel Analysis").

Paragraph 5

Pillar is not alone in thinking Iraq has worsened the terrorist problem. A growing number of politicians, statesmen, and reporters have come to the same conclusion. Perhaps most damning was an authoritative intelligence report partially released in 2006, called *Trends in Global Terrorism: Implications for the United States*. The report combined the views of sixteen government agencies and concluded that the war in Iraq had unequivocally increased the terrorist threat. The report caused Senator Edward Kennedy to say, "The intelligence community has reported the plain truth— the misguided war in Iraq has metastasized and spread terrorism like cancer around the world." Other politicians, including Senator Jay Rockefeller, Congressman John Murtha, and Senator Harry Reid, have joined Kennedy in saying the Iraq War has served to ignite, rather than stem, the flames of terrorism.

This quote was taken from the quote box that accompanies Viewpoint Two. When you see particularly striking quotes, save them to use to support points in your essays.

Paragraph 6

Why has the war in Iraq increased terrorism both in that country and abroad? Many experts think that Iraq has become a focal point of terrorism and an exporter of terrorists because it symbolizes for people the ways in which the United States has imperialistic aims to control the people of the Middle East and their oil. In other words, a lot of people hate the United States because they think it wants to control other countries and take their resources; the debacle in Iraq is all but proving such views correct. Indeed, the United States has no timetable for leaving Iraq; had allowed its corporations such as Bechtel to engage in multi-decades long contracts to profit from Iraq's oil industry; and the military has proposed setting up permanent bases there. Those who resent the United States' intru-

What is the topic sentence of paragraph 6? (Hint: It is not the first sentence.)

Which of the author's points does this sentence help prove?

sion into the affairs of Iraq, and the broader Middle East, thus see terrorism as a just way to fight against what they think are attempts by the United States to control the region indefinitely.

Paragraph 7

Another reason why Iraq has become a hot spot for terrorism is because it offers a chaotic, violent, and tension-filled environment in which terrorists can comfortably operate and find allies. In Iraq, those willing to die or kill others for a cause they believe in are plentiful. One Iraqi insurgency leader, Abu Nour, attested to this fact in a 2006 interview with a journalist he kidnapped. Nour, who has led hundreds of terrorist attacks in Iraq, said, "I have maybe 2,000 mujahadeen [soldiers] in all Iraq, in all towns. If I divide this into groups of 20, I have 100 groups. So this means I have 100 operations in a week. So in a month I have 400 operations. So if in every operation I kill only 2 soldiers, I kill 800 soldiers in a month" (qtd. in Carroll). Clearly, there is no shortage of people willing to commit terrorism in Iraq.

> Make a list of all the transitions that appear in the essay and how they keep the ideas flowing.

Paragraph 8

Its manifestation of U.S. imperialism and its chaotic conditions are just a few reasons why Iraq has become a breeding ground for terrorism. One reporter with thorough knowledge of Iraq succinctly explains a few other reasons why the bungled war in Iraq is perfect fuel for the terrorists' cause: "So far the war in Iraq has advanced the jihadist cause because it generates a steady supply of Islamic victims, or martyrs; because it seems to prove Osama bin Laden's contention that America lusts to occupy Islam's sacred sites, abuse Muslim people, and steal Muslim resources; and because it raises the tantalizing possibility that humble Muslim insurgents, with cheap, primitive weapons, can once more hobble and ultimately destroy a superpower" (Fallows 69). Indeed, the chance to take up arms against what they believe is a great oppressor has been one of the enduring appeals of the insurgency force operating in Iraq.

> Analyze this quote. What do you think made the author want to select it for inclusion in the essay?

How does the author avoid repeating what has been stated elsewhere in the essay?

What was once undertaken in an effort to curb the spread of terrorism has instead unleashed terrorism's dark force around the globe. American policy makers must not be blind to the fact that the war in Iraq has increased terrorism. In fact, they should realize that since terrorism is largely fueled by a hatred of America's occupation of Middle Eastern lands, the key to preventing terrorism could be simply to end these campaigns of occupation. Terrorism expert Robert A. Pape is one of many voices that argue the best way to prevent terrorism is to get the United States out of Iraq. "The longer our forces stay on the ground in the Arabian Peninsula," warns Pape, "the greater the risk of the next 9/11, whether that is a suicide attack, a nuclear attack, or a biological attack" (qtd. in McConnell). To keep Americans truly safe, U.S. officials must realize that the Iraq War has worsened the terrorist problem and begin to solve the problem from that perspective.

After reading this essay, did the author persuade you to agree with her point of view? If so, what pieces of evidence swayed you? If not, why not?

Works Cited

Carroll, Jill. "An Interview with an Iraqi insurgent." *Christian Science Monitor* 22 Aug. 2006 < www.csmonitor.com/2006/0822/p11s02-woiq.html > .

Fallows, James. "Declaring Victory." *Atlantic* Sept. 2006: 60–73.

McConnell, Scott. "It's the Occupation, Not the Fundamentalism." *American Conservative* 18 July 2005.

Nordland, Rod. "Terror for Export." *Newsweek* 21 Nov. 2005: 38.

"Rumsfeld Skeptical of Intel Analysis: Secretary Says It's Impossible to Know Whether Wars Created More Terror." *CBSNews.com* 26 Sept. 2006 < www.cbsnews.com/stories/2006/09/27/terror/main2042311.shtml > .

Statement by Senator Edward M. Kennedy. "New National Intelligence Estimate Determines That the Misguided War Has 'Metastasized and Spread' Terrorism." 23 Sept. 2006 < http://kennedy.senate.gov/newsroom/press_release.cfm?id = ff5e05ad-8e48-447f-a015-c3ef25303548 > .

Exercise 3A: Examining Introductions and Conclusions

Every essay features introductory and concluding paragraphs that are used to frame the main ideas being presented. Along with presenting the essay's thesis statement, well-written introductions should grab the attention of the reader and make clear why the topic being explored is important. The conclusion reiterates the essay's thesis and is also the last chance for the writer to make an impression on the reader. Strong introductions and conclusions can greatly enhance an essay's effect on an audience.

The Introduction

There are several techniques that can be used to craft an introductory paragraph. An essay can start with

- an anecdote: a brief story that illustrates a point relevant to the topic;
- startling information: facts or statistics that elucidate the point of the essay;
- setting up and knocking down a position: a position or claim believed by proponents of one side of a controversy, followed by statements that challenge that claim;
- historical perspective: an example of the way things used to be that leads into a discussion of how or why things work differently now;
- summary information: general introductory information about the topic that feeds into the essay's thesis statement.

1. Reread the introductory paragraphs of the model essays and of the viewpoints in Section One. Identify which of the techniques described above are used in the example essays. How do they grab the attention of the reader? Are thesis statements clearly presented?

2. Write an introduction for the essay you have outlined and partially written in Exercise 1B using one of the techniques described above.

The Conclusion

The conclusion brings the essay to a close by summarizing or returning to its main ideas. Good conclusions, however, go beyond simply repeating these ideas. Strong conclusions explore a topic's broader implications and reiterate why it is important to consider. They may frame the essay by returning to an anecdote featured in the opening paragraph. Or they may close with a quotation or refer to an event in the essay. In opinionated essays, the conclusion can reiterate which side the essay is taking or ask the reader to reconsider a previously held position on the subject.

3. Reread the concluding paragraphs of the model essays and of the viewpoints in Section One. Which were most effective in driving their arguments home to the reader? What sorts of techniques did they use to do this? Did they appeal emotionally to the reader, or bookend an idea or event referenced elsewhere in the essay?

4. Write a conclusion for the essay you have outlined and partially written in Exercise 1B using one of the techniques described above.

Exercise 3B: Using Quotations to Enliven Your Essay

No essay is complete without quotations. Get in the habit of using quotes to support at least some of the ideas in your essays. Quotes do not need to appear in every paragraph, but often enough so that the essay contains voices aside from your own. When you write, use quotations to accomplish the following:

- Provide expert advice that you are not necessarily in the position to know about.
- Cite lively or passionate passages.
- Include a particularly well-written point that gets to the heart of the matter.
- Supply statistics or facts that have been derived from someone's research.

- Deliver anecdotes that illustrate the point you are trying to make.
- Express first-person testimony.

Problem One:
Reread the essays presented in all sections of this book and find at least one example of each of the above quotation types.

There are a couple of important things to remember when using quotations:

- Note your sources' qualifications and biases. This way your reader can identify the person you have quoted and can put their words in a context.
- Put any quoted material within proper quotation marks. Failing to attribute quotes to their authors constitutes plagiarism, which is when an author takes someone else's words or ideas and presents them as his or her own. Plagiarism is a very serious infraction and must be avoided at all costs.

Write Your Own Persuasive Five-Paragraph Essay

Using the information from this book, write your own five-paragraph persuasive essay that deals with the Iraq War. You can use the resources in this book for information about issues relating to this topic and how to structure this type of essay.

The following steps are suggestions on how to get started.

Step One: Choose your topic.
The first step is to decide what topic to write your persuasive essay on. Is there any subject that particularly fascinates you about the Iraq War? Is there an issue you strongly support, or feel strongly against? Is there a topic you feel personally connected to or one that you would like to learn more about? Ask yourself such questions before selecting your essay topic. Refer to Appendix D: Sample Essay Topics if you need help selecting a topic.

Step Two: Write down questions and answers about the topic.
Before you begin writing, you will need to think carefully about what ideas your essay will contain. This is a process known as *brainstorming*. Brainstorming involves asking yourself questions and coming up with ideas to discuss in your essay. Possible questions that will help you with the brainstorming process include:

- Why is this topic important?
- Why should people be interested in this topic?
- How can I make this essay interesting to the reader?
- What question am I going to address in this paragraph or essay?
- What facts, ideas, or quotes can I use to support the answer to my question?

Questions especially for persuasive essays include:
- Is there something I want to convince my reader of?
- Is there a topic I want to advocate in favor of, or rally against?

- Is there enough evidence to support my opinion?
- Do I want to make a call to action—motivate my readers to do something about a particular problem or event?

Step Three: Gather facts, ideas, and anecdotes related to your topic.

This book contains several places to find information about many aspects of the Iraq War, including the viewpoints and the appendixes. In addition, you may want to research the books, articles, and Web sites listed in Section Three, or do additional research in your local library. You can also conduct interviews if you know someone who has a compelling story that would fit well in your essay.

Step Four: Develop a workable thesis statement.

Use what you have written down in steps two and three to help you articulate the main point or argument you want to make in your essay. It should be expressed in a clear sentence and make an arguable or supportable point.

Example:

Many can agree U.S. forces have a difficult time stabilizing Iraq; but all our efforts will be for naught if the troops are withdrawn before the job is done.
This could be the thesis statement of a persuasive essay that argues the United States should not leave Iraq before the country is stabilized. Supporting paragraphs would explore reasons why the author thinks this is a good course of action.

Step Five: Write an outline or diagram.

1. Write the thesis statement at the top of the outline.
2. Write roman numerals I, II, and III on the left side of the page with A, B, and C under each numeral.
3. Next to each roman numeral, write down the best ideas you came up with in step three. These should all directly relate to and support the thesis statement.
4. Next to each letter write down information that supports that particular idea.

Step Six: Write the three supporting paragraphs.
Use your outline to write the three supporting paragraphs. Write down the main idea of each paragraph in sentence form. Do the same thing for the supporting points of information. Each sentence should support the paragraph of the topic. Be sure you have relevant and interesting details, facts, and quotes. Use transitions when you move from idea to idea to keep the text fluid and smooth. Sometimes, although not always, paragraphs can include a concluding or summary sentence that restates the paragraph's argument.

Step Seven: Write the introduction and conclusion.
See Exercise 3A for information on writing introductions and conclusions.

Step Eight: Read and rewrite.
As you read, check your essay for the following:

✔ Does the essay maintain a consistent tone?

✔ Do all paragraphs reinforce your general thesis?

✔ Do all paragraphs flow from one to the other? Do you need to add transition words or phrases?

✔ Have you quoted from reliable, authoritative, and interesting sources?

✔ Is there a sense of progression throughout the essay?

✔ Does the essay get bogged down in too much detail or irrelevant material?

✔ Does your introduction grab the reader's attention?

✔ Does your conclusion reflect on any previously discussed material, or give the essay a sense of closure?

✔ Are there any spelling or grammatical errors?

Section Three:
Supporting
Research
Material

Time Line of the Iraq War

Editor's Note: These facts contained in this time line can be used in reports or papers to reinforce or add credibility when making important points or claims.

March 2003
The Iraq War begins on March 19 when U.S. forces invade.

April 2003
In an emotional and symbolic moment, a statue of Saddam Hussein is toppled in Baghdad on April 9 by Iraqis with the help of U.S. forces, signifying the fall of the nation's capital.

May 2003
President Bush declares the mission in Iraq as "accomplished" on May 1 and says that major combat operations are over. Troops remain in Iraq to secure remaining sectors of the country.

July 2003
Bush challenges insurgent fighters to attack U.S. soldiers: "There are some who feel like—that the conditions are such that they can attack us there. My answer is: bring them on."

The number of U.S. combat deaths reaches 147, the same number as in the Gulf War.

August 2003
On August 20 the UN headquarters in Baghdad is attacked by insurgents, killing at least seventeen people.

November 2003
On November 14, General John Abizaid, head of U.S. Central Command, estimates the number of insurgent fighters at no more than five thousand.

December 2003
Saddam Hussein is captured by U.S. forces on December 13.

January 2004
Five hundred soldiers have been killed since the beginning of the invasion.

Because of tensions and power struggles between Iraq's ethnic groups, CIA officers warn that Iraq is on the path toward a civil war.

March 2004
Former chief UN weapons inspector Hans Blix declares the war in Iraq to be illegal.

April 2004
Reporters break the Abu Ghraib scandal, in which U.S. forces were found to have tortured Iraqi prisoners of war.

May 2004
American contractor Nicholas Berg is beheaded by Iraqi militants. Video of his violent death circulates on the Internet.

June 2004
U.S. officially transfers sovereignty to Iraqi leaders, but troops remain in the country to provide security and train Iraqi police forces.

July 2004
Congress votes to continue funding in Iraq.

September 2004
The number of U.S. troops killed in Iraq reaches one thousand.

October 2004
The British journal the *Lancet* estimates that one hundred thousand Iraqis have died as a result of the war.

January 2005

Iraqi intelligence director General Mohamed Abdullah Shahwani estimates the force of the insurgency to number around forty thousand fighters, with two hundred thousand active supporters.

A Zogby poll shows 82 percent of Sunni Arabs and 69 percent of Shiites want a U.S. withdrawal immediately, or after an elected government is in place.

Weapons inspectors officially end their search for weapons of mass destruction in Iraq. To date no weapons of mass destruction of the type the Bush administration claimed were owned by Saddam Hussein have been found by international inspection agencies.

March 2005

A hunger specialist from the UN estimates that child malnutrition in Iraq has almost doubled since the U.S. invasion.

May 2005

Vice President Dick Cheney argues the insurgency is in what he calls its "last throes."

August 2005

A poll taken by the British Ministry of Defense finds that 82 percent of Iraqis are strongly opposed to the presence of coalition troops; less than 1 percent believe coalition forces are responsible for any improvement in security; 67 percent feel less secure as a result of the U.S. occupation; and 72 percent do not have confidence in multinational forces.

October 2005

The number of U.S. troops killed in Iraq reaches two thousand.

December 2005

Iraqi elections are held to elect members of the Iraqi Assembly. The United Iraqi Alliance, the Shiite Muslim's most powerful party, wins a majority of the seats.

January 2006

A World Public Opinion poll finds 80 percent of Iraqis believe the United States will have permanent military bases in Iraq, and that 47 percent of Iraqis support attacks against occupying forces.

February 2006

A bomb is detonated inside a major Shiite Muslim shrine, setting off a wave of sectarian violence.

March 2006

Senator Tom Harkin declares the situation has deteriorated into "civil war."

An AP-Ipsos poll finds that the majority of Americans believe civil war will break out in Iraq.

April 2006

Jawad al-Maliki becomes prime minister of Iraq.

May 2006

The Pentagon reports that the frequency of insurgent attacks against occupation troops and Iraqi civilians is at its highest level since it began tracking such figures in 2004.

Prime Minister Maliki oversees the formation of Iraq's first permanent constitutional government since the fall of Saddam Hussein.

June 2006

Abu Musab al-Zarqawi, the leader of al Qaeda in Iraq, is killed during a U.S. air raid.

A UN agency, UN Assistance Mission for Iraq (UNAMI), estimates that 1.3 million Iraqis have been displaced as a result of the war.

The number of U.S. soldiers killed in conflict reaches twenty-five hundred.

The U.S. Senate approves a $509 billion military budget. It includes $50 billion for military violence in Afghanistan and Iraq.

A Harris Interactive poll finds 61 percent of people in the U.S. believe "Invading and occupying Iraq has motivated more Islamic terrorists to attack Americans and the United States."

A *New York Times*/CBS News poll finds 71 percent of people in the United States believe occupying Iraq for several more years would either make no difference in their security or make them less safe.

August 2006

In this month 3,438 Iraqi civilians are killed, making it the deadliest month of the war for Iraqi civilians.

A total of 1,666 bombs explode in Iraq, the highest monthly total for the war.

The war has lasted 1,249 days—longer than World War II.

September 2006

According to Department of Defense statistics, 2,662 soldiers have been killed. This number does not include journalists, relief workers, or contractors who have been killed.

Iraq becomes the deadliest place for journalists to work. A new study by the Committee to Protect Journalists finds that of the 580 journalists who have been killed over the last fifteen years, 78 died in Iraq.

A National Intelligence Estimate report that is the product of sixteen government agencies' analyses of Iraq finds that the Iraq War has increased the threat of terrorism.

A World Opinion poll finds that 71 percent of Iraqis want the United States to withdraw within one year.

October 2006

The UN reports that 914,000 Iraqis have fled from their homes since the March 2003 invasion of Iraq.

It is estimated by researchers at Johns Hopkins University that 655,000 Iraqi civilians have died as a result of the U.S. invasion.

A CNN poll finds that 58 percent of Americans believe the Bush administration has deliberately misled the American public about the war in Iraq.

Utility service in Baghdad reaches record low levels. Residents of Baghdad receive an average of 2.4 hours of electricity, compared to an average of 16 to 24 hours of electricity before the war began.

November 2006
Reports indicate that a record number of Iraqis are killed in October 2006 in sectarian violence.

A classified U.S. government report finds that the Iraqi insurgency is so powerful it is able to raise tens of millions of dollars annually through activities such as oil smuggling, kidnapping, counterfeiting, corrupt charities, and other crimes.

NBC decides to refer to the conflict in Iraq as a "civil war."

December 2006
Saddam Hussein is executed by hanging.

The Iraqi Study Group is made up of high-level American diplomats, politicians, and academics. Its recommendations include refraining from seeking permanent military bases in Iraq, pursuing diplomacy with militia and insurgent leaders, and avoiding keeping the American troop force in Iraq indefinitely.

January 2007
President Bush's approval rating drops to 28 percent, a career low, according to a CBS poll. The same poll finds 66 percent opposition to escalating the war in Iraq, and 75 percent who think the war is going badly.

At more than three thousand, the total number of American dead in Iraq surpasses the number of Americans killed in the September 11 attacks.

President Bush, in an attempt to escalate the conflict in order to finish it, commits to sending an additional twenty thousand troops to Iraq. Seventy percent of Americans oppose the move.

The Iraq War reaches a cost of $8.4 billion per month.

March 2007
The fifth anniversary of the Iraq War arrives with 3,229 troops killed, along with hundreds of thousands of Iraqis.

For the first time since the Iraq War began, a CNN poll finds that less than half of Americans (46 percent) believe the United States can win in Iraq.

The Pentagon acknowledges that Iraq is caught in civil war.

April 2007
The Iraqi Parliament is bombed in a suicide attack.

September 2007
U.S. troop fatalities in Iraq reached 3,771, according to the Department of Defense. Iraqi civilian casualties, which the Defense Department does not count, are approximately 71,000 to 78,000. Other estimates put the number of Iraqi dead as high as 655,000.

Finding and Using Sources of Information

No matter what type of essay you are writing, it is necessary to find information to support your point of view. You can use sources such as books, magazine articles, newspaper articles, and online articles.

Using Books and Articles

You can find books and articles in a library by using the library's computer or cataloging system. If you are not sure how to use these resources, ask a librarian to help you. You can also use a computer to find many magazine articles and other articles written specifically for the Internet.

You are likely to find a lot more information than you can possibly use in your essay, so your first task is to narrow it down to what is likely to be most usable. Look at book and article titles. Look at book chapter titles, and examine the book's index to see if it contains information on the specific topic you want to write about. (For example, if you want to write about weapons of mass destruction in Iraq and you find a book about the war in general, check the chapter titles and index to be sure it contains information about weapons of mass destruction before you bother to check out the book.)

For a five-paragraph essay, you do not need a great deal of supporting information, so quickly try to narrow down your materials to a few good books and magazine or Internet articles. You do not need dozens. You might even find that one or two good books or articles contain all the information you need.

You probably do not have time to read an entire book, so find the chapters or sections that relate to your topic, and skim these. When you find useful information, copy it onto a note card or notebook. You should look for supporting facts, statistics, quotations, and examples.

Using the Internet

When you select your supporting information, it is important that you evaluate its source. This is especially important with information you find on the Internet. Because nearly anyone can put information on the Internet, there is as much bad information as good information. Before using Internet information—or any information—try to determine if the source seems to be reliable. Is the author or Internet site sponsored by a legitimate organization? Is it from a government source? Does the author have any special knowledge or training relating to the topic you are looking up? Does the article give any indication of where its information comes from?

Using Your Supporting Information

When you use supporting information from a book, article, interview, or other source, there are three important things to remember:

1. *Make it clear whether you are using a direct quotation or a paraphrase.* If you copy information directly from your source, you are quoting it. You must put quotation marks around the information, and tell where the information comes from. If you put the information in your own words, you are paraphrasing it.

   Here is an example of using a quotation:
   Author James Dobbins believes that the Bush administration's handling of the Iraq War has doomed it to failure in that country. Explains Dobbins: "The ongoing war in Iraq is not one that the United States can win. As a result of its initial miscalculations, misdirected planning, and inadequate preparation, Washington has lost the Iraqi people's confidence and consent, and it is unlikely to win them back. Every day that Americans shell Iraqi cities they lose further ground on the central front of Iraqi opinion" (16).

Here is an example of a brief paraphrase of the same passage:

Author James Dobbins believes that the Bush administration's handling of the Iraq War has doomed it to failure in that country. Dobbins believes that because the administration miscalculated what would be required to secure the country and failed to predict the complex problems that would spring up after the invasion, they lost the confidence of the Iraqi people—and will be unable to get it back as long as the violence continues.

2. *Use the information fairly.* Be careful to use supporting information in the way the author intended it. For example, it is unfair to quote an author as saying, "Iraqi civilians have enjoyed a high quality of life following the U.S. invasion," when he or she intended to say, "Iraqi civilians have enjoyed a high quality of life following the U.S. invasion—that is, if high rates of murder, kidnapping, extortion, and lack of clean water and electricity is your idea of a vacation." This is called taking information out of context. This is using supporting evidence unfairly.

3. *Give credit where credit is due.* Giving credit is known as citing. You must use citations when you use someone else's information, but not every piece of supporting information needs a citation.

   - If the supporting information is general knowledge—that is, it can be found in many sources—you do not have to cite your source.

   - If you directly quote a source, you must cite it.

   - If you paraphrase information from a specific source, you must cite it.

If you do not use citations where you should, you are *plagiarizing*—or stealing—someone else's work.

Citing Your Sources

There are a number of ways to cite your sources. Your teacher will probably want you to do it in one of three ways:

- Informal: As in the example in number 1 above, tell where you got the information as you present it in the text of your essay.

- Informal list: At the end of your essay, place an unnumbered list of all the sources you used. This tells the reader where, in general, your information came from.

- Formal: Use numbered footnotes or endnotes. Footnotes or endnotes are generally placed at the end of an article or essay, although they may be placed elsewhere depending on your teacher's requirements.

Work Cited

Dobbins, James. "Iraq: Winning the Unwinnable War." *Foreign Affairs* Jan/Feb 2005: 16.

Using MLA Style to Create a Works Cited List

You will probably need to create a list of works cited for your paper. These include materials that you quoted from, relied heavily on, or consulted to write your paper. There are several different ways to structure these references. The following examples are based on Modern Language Association (MLA) style, one of the major citation styles used by writers.

Book Entries

For most book entries you will need the author's name, the book's title, where it was published, what company published it, and the year it was published. This information is usually found on the inside of the book. Variations on book entries include the following:

A book by a single author:
> Afrasiabi, Kaveh. *Iran's Nuclear Program: Debating Facts Versus Fiction*. Charleston, SC: BookSurge, 2006.

Two or more books by the same author:
> Friedman, Thomas L. *From Beirut to Jerusalem*. New York: Doubleday, 1989.
> ———, *The World Is Flat: A Brief History of the Twentieth Century*. New York: Farrar, Straus and Giroux, 2005.

A book by two or more authors:
> Pojman, Louis P., and Jeffrey Reiman. *The Death Penalty: For and Against*. Lanham, MD: Rowman & Littlefield, 1998.

A book with an editor:
> Friedman, Lauri S., ed. *Introducing Issues with Opposing Viewpoints: Weapons of Mass Destruction*. Farmington Hills, MI: Greenhaven, 2006.

Periodical and Newspaper Entries

Entries for sources found in periodicals and newspapers are cited a bit differently from books. For one, these sources usually have a title and a publication name. They also may have specific dates and page numbers. Unlike book entries, you do not need to list where newspapers or periodicals are published or what company publishes them.

An article from a periodical:
> Zakaria, Fareed. "Let Them Eat Carrots." *Newsweek* 23 Oct. 2004: 42.

An unsigned article from a periodical:
> "Going Critical, Defying the World." *Economist* 21 Oct. 2004: 70.

An article from a newspaper:
> McCain, John. "The War You're Not Reading About." *Washington Post* 8 Apr. 2007: B07.

Internet Sources

To document a source you found online, try to provide as much information on it as possible, including the author's name, the title of the document, date of publication or of last revision, the URL, and your date of access.

A Web source:
> Shyovitz, David. "The History and Development of Yiddish." Jewish Virtual Library. 30 May 2005 < http://www.jewishvirtuallibrary.org/jsource/History/yiddish.html > . Accessed 2007. Sept. 4

Your teacher will tell you exactly how information should be cited in your essay. Generally, the very least information needed is the original author's name and the name of the article or other publication.

Be sure you know exactly what information your teacher requires before you start looking for your supporting information so that you know what information to include with your notes.

Sample Essay Topics

The United States Can Win the Iraq War

The United States Cannot Win the Iraq War

The United States Should Withdraw Immediately from Iraq

The United States Cannot Withdraw from Iraq Yet

The United States Should Avoid Setting a Timetable for Withdrawal from Iraq

The Iraq War Was Worth Fighting

The Iraq War Was Not Worth Fighting

Iraq Is Headed for a Civil War

Iraq Is Not Headed for a Civil War

The Iraq War Was Key to the War on Terror

The Iraq War Was Unrelated to the War on Terror

Democracy Will Succeed in Iraq

Democracy Will Not Succeed in Iraq

The Lives of Iraqi Civilians Have Improved as a Result of the Iraq War

The Lives of Iraqi Civilians Have Worsened as a Result of the Iraq War

The Media Prefers to Tell Bad News About Iraq

The Media Does Not Report Enough Bad News About Iraq

The Bush Administration Misled the American Public on the Threat Posed by Iraq

The Bush Administration Did Not Mislead the American Public on the Threat Posed by Iraq

The Iraqi Insurgency Is Comprised of Homegrown Terrorists

The Iraqi Insurgency Draws Fighters from Around the Globe

Iraq Had Weapons of Mass Destruction

Iraq Did Not Have Weapons of Mass Destruction

Organizations to Contact

The editors have compiled the following list of organizations concerned with the issues debated in this book. The descriptions are derived from materials provided by the organizations. All have publications or information available for interested readers. The list was compiled on the date of publication of the present volume; names, addresses, and phone numbers may change. Be aware that many organizations take several weeks or longer to respond to inquiries, so allow as much time as possible.

American Enterprise Institute (AEI)
1150 Seventeenth St. NW, Washington, DC 20036 • (202) 862-5800 • fax: (202) 862-7177 • Web site: www.aei.org

The American Enterprise Institute for Public Policy Research is a scholarly research institute that is dedicated to preserving limited government, private enterprise, and a strong foreign policy and national defense. It publishes books, including *Democratic Realism: An American Foreign Policy for a Unipolar World* and *The Islamic Paradox: Shiite Clerics, Sunni Fundamentalists, and the Coming of Arab Democracy*, and a bimonthly magazine, *American Enterprise*.

The Brookings Institution
1775 Massachusetts Ave. NW, Washington, DC 20036 • (202) 797-6000 • fax: (202) 797-6004 • e-mail: brookinfo@ brook.edu • Web site: www.brookings.org

The institution, founded in 1927, is a think tank that conducts research and education in foreign policy, economics, government, and the social sciences. In 2001 it began America's Response to Terrorism, a project that provides briefings and analysis to the public and which is featured on the center's Web site. Its publishes the quarterly *Brookings Review*, periodic *Policy Briefs*, and books on Middle Eastern countries, including Iraq.

CATO Institute

1000 Massachusetts Ave. NW, Washington, DC 20001-5403
(202) 842-0200 • fax: (202) 842-3490 • e-mail: cato@cato.org
Web site: www.cato.org

The CATO Institute is a nonpartisan public policy research foundation dedicated to limiting the role of government and protecting individual liberties. It publishes the quarterly magazine *Regulation*, the bimonthly *Cato Policy Report*, and numerous policy papers and articles.

Center for Middle Eastern Studies

University of Texas, Austin, TX 78712 • (512) 471-3881 • fax: (512) 471-7834 • e-mail: cmes@menic.texas.edu • Web site: http://menic.utexas.edu/menic/cmes

The center was established by the U.S. Department of Education to promote a better understanding of the Middle East. It provides research and instructional materials and publishes three series of books on the Middle East: the Modern Middle East series, the Middle East Monograph series, and the Modern Middle East Literatures in Translation series.

Center for Strategic and International Studies (CSIS)

1800 K St. NW, Suite 400, Washington, DC 20006 • (202) 887-0200 • fax: (202) 775-3199 • Web site: www.csis.org

The center works to provide world leaders with strategic insights and policy options on current and emerging global issues. It publishes books, including *The "Instant" Lessons of the Iraq War*, the *Washington Quarterly*, a journal on political, economic, and security issues, and other publications, including reports that can be downloaded from its Web site.

Council on Foreign Relations

58 E. Sixty-eighth St., New York, NY 10021 • (212) 434-9400 fax: (212) 434-9800 • e-mail: communications@cfr.org
Web site: www.cfr.org

The council researches the international aspects of American economic and political policies. Its journal *Foreign Affairs*, published five times a year, provides analysis on global conflicts, including the Iraq War.

Education for Peace in Iraq Center (EPIC)

1101 Pennsylvania Ave. SE, Washington, DC 20003 • (202) 543-6176 • e-mail: info@epic-use.org • Web site: http://epic-usa.org/

The organization works to improve humanitarian conditions in Iraq and protect the human rights of Iraq's people. It opposed both international economic sanctions and U.S. military action against Iraq. Articles on Iraq are available on its Web site.

Hoover Institution

Stanford University, Stanford, CA 94305-6010 • (650) 723-1754 • fax: (650) 723-1687 • Web site: www.hoover.stanford.edu/

The Hoover Institution is a public policy research center devoted to advanced study of politics, economics, and political economy—both domestic and foreign—as well as international affairs. It publishes the quarterly *Hoover Digest*, which often includes articles on Iraq, the Middle East, and the war on terrorism, as well as a newsletter and special reports.

Human Rights Watch (HRW)

485 Fifth Ave., New York, NY 10017-6104 • (212) 972-8400 fax: (212) 972-0905 • e-mail: hrwnyc@hrw.org • Web site: www.hrw.org

HRW regularly investigates human rights abuses in over seventy countries around the world. It promotes civil liberties and defends freedom of thought, due process, and the equal protection of the law. Its goal is to hold governments accountable for human rights violations they commit against individuals because of their political, ethnic, or religious affiliations. It publishes a wealth of information about Iraq, including current information, background information, and regular human rights reports.

The Iraq Foundation

1012 Fourteenth St. NW, Suite 1110, Washington, DC 20005 (202) 347-4662 • fax: (202) 347-7897 and 7898 • e-mail: iraq@iraqfoundation.org • Web site: www.iraqfoundation.org

The Iraq Foundation is a nonprofit, nongovernmental organization working for democracy and human rights in Iraq and for a better international understanding of Iraq's potential as a contributor to political stability and economic progress in the Middle East. Information on its projects as well as other information on Iraq can be found on its Web site.

Middle East Policy Council (MEPC)

1730 M St. NW, Suite 512, Washington, DC 20036 • (202) 296-6767 • fax: (202) 296-5791 • e-mail: info@mepc.org Web site: www.mepc.org

The purpose of this nonprofit organization is to contribute to an understanding of current issues in U.S. relations with countries of the Middle East. It publishes the quarterly journal *Middle East Policy* as well as special reports and books.

Middle East Studies Association

University of Arizona, 1643 E. Helen St., Tucson, AZ 85721 (520) 621-5850 • fax: (520) 626-9095 • e-mail: mesana@u. arizona.edu • Web site: http://w3fp.arizona.edu/mesassoc/

This professional academic association of scholars on the Middle East focuses particularly on the rise of Islam. It publishes the quarterly *International Journal of Middle East Studies* and runs a project for the evaluation of textbooks for coverage of the Middle East.

The National Endowment for Democracy (NED)

1101 Fifteenth Street NW, Suite 700, Washington, DC 20005 (202) 293-9072 • fax: (202) 223-6042 • e-mail: info@ned.org

The NED is a private, nonprofit organization created in 1983 to strengthen democratic institutions around the world through nongovernmental efforts. It publishes the bimonthly periodical *Journal of Democracy*.

U.N. Development Programme (UNDP) in Iraq

One United Nations Plaza, New York, NY 10017 • (212) 906-5317 • Web site: www.iq.undp.org/

UNDP is the United Nations' global development network, helping countries build solutions to the challenges of democratic governance, poverty reduction, crisis prevention and recovery, energy and environment, information and communications technology, and HIV/AIDS. The UNDP has been present in Iraq since 1976.

U.S. Department of State, Bureau of Near Eastern Affairs

2201 C St. NW, Washington, DC 20520 • (202) 647-4000
Web site: www.state.gov/p/nea/

The bureau deals with U.S. foreign policy and U.S. relations with the countries in the Middle East, including Iraq. Its Web site offers country information as well as news briefings and press statements on U.S. foreign policy.

Women's Alliance for Democracy in Iraq (WAFDI)

1730 Arlington Blvd., Arlington, VA 22209 • e-mail: sarbagh salih@cs.com • Web site: www.wafdi.org

WAFDI is an international nonpartisan and not-for-profit women's rights organization. WAFDI is dedicated to a free and democratic Iraq with full and equal individual rights for women. The organization is committed to the advancement and empowerment of women in all areas of society including but not limited to family, economics, education, health, arts, literature, sports, and politics.

Bibliography

Books

Allawi, Ali A., *The Occupation of Iraq: Winning the War, Losing the Peace.* New Haven, CT: Yale University Press, 2007.

Baker III, James A., and Lee H. Hamilton, *The Iraq Study Group Report: The Way Forward—a New Approach.* New York: Vintage, 2006.

Brigham, Robert K., *Is Iraq Another Vietnam?* New York: Public Affairs, 2006.

Buzzell, Colby, *My War: Killing Time in Iraq.* Berkley Trade, 2006.

Galbraith, Peter W., *The End of Iraq: How American Incompetence Created a War Without End.* New York: Simon & Schuster, 2006.

Gardner, Lloyd, and Marilyn B. Young, eds., *Iraq and the Lessons of Vietnam: Or, How Not to Learn from the Past.* New York: New Press, 2007.

Greeley, Andrew M., *A Stupid, Unjust, and Criminal War: Iraq 2001–2007.* New York: 2007.

Hafez, Mohammed M., *Suicide Bombers in Iraq: The Strategy and Ideology of Martyrdom.* Washington, DC: United States Institute of Peace Press, 2007.

Hashim, Ahmed S., *Insurgency and Counter-Insurgency in Iraq.* Ithaca, NY: Cornell University Press, 2006.

Hayden, Tom, *Ending the War in Iraq.* New York: Akashic, 2007.

Ricks, Thomas E., *Fiasco: The American Military Adventure in Iraq.* New York: Penguin, 2006.

Tripp, Charles, *A History of Iraq.* Cambridge: Cambridge University Press, 2007.

Periodicals

Baird, Jonathan P., "Why We Must Leave Iraq." *New Hampshire Business Review* 5 Jan. 2007: 20.

Basham, Patrick, "Can Iraq Be Democratic? *Policy Analysis* 5 Jan. 2004.

Bergen, Peter, and Paul Cruickshank, "Iraq 101: The Iraq Effect—the War in Iraq and Its Impact on the War on Terrorism." *Mother Jones* 1 Mar. 2007 < http://www.motherjones.com/news/featurex/2007/03/iraq_effect_1.html > .

Black, Edwin, "Given Its History, Can We Succeed in Iraq?" *History News Network* 27 Dec. 2004.

Brownback, Sam, "Brownback Makes Statement on Iraq." 9 Feb. 2007 < http://brownback.senate.gov/pressapp/record.cfm?id = 269089 > .

Carr, David, "Iraq: What We're Not Seeing." *New York Times Upfront* 9 Oct. 2006.

Country Reports on Terrorism, U.S. Department of State 2006 < http://www.state.gov/s/ct/rls/crt/2006 > .

Dagher, Sam, "Is Baghdad Safer? Yes and No." *Christian Science Monitor* 13 Apr. 2007 < www.csmonitor.com/2007/0413/p01s04-woiq.html > .

Dobbins, James, "Iraq: Winning the Unwinnable War." *Foreign Affairs* Jan.–Feb. 2005: 16.

Fallows, James, "Declaring Victory." *Atlantic* Sept. 2006.

Fearon, James D., "Iraq's Civil War." *Foreign Affairs* Mar.–Apr. 2007.

Finkel, David, "Beyond Iraq: The Spreading Crisis." *Against the Current* 21 May/June 2006: 26.

Ghosh, Aparisim, "Inside the Mind of an Iraqi Suicide Bomber." *Time* 4 July 2005.

Glazov, Jamie, "Symposium: The War for the Soul of Iraq." *FrontPageMagazine.com* 2 Dec. 2005.

Hanson, Victor Davis, "Why We Must Stay in Iraq." *Washington Post* 4 Sept. 2005.

Herman, Arthur, "How to Win in Iraq—and How to Lose." *Commentary* April 2007 < www.commentarymagazine.com/cm/main/viewArticle.html?id = 108567 > .

Hitchens, Christopher, "Which Iraq War Do You Want to End? We're Fighting at Least Three of Them." *Slate.com,* 27 Aug. 2007 < www.slate.com/id/2172904 > .

Howell, Llewellyn D., "Withdrawal Will Require Smart Strategizing." *Star Bulletin* (Honolulu) 9 Oct. 2005 < http://starbulletin.com/2005/10/09/editorial/special.html > .

"Iraqis' Daily Lives," *BBC.com* 7Apr. 2006 < http://news. bbc.co.uk/2/hi/middle_east/4881164.stm > .

Leaver, Erik, "Top 10 Reasons for the US to Get Out of Iraq." *Nation* 11 Oct. 2004 < www.thenation.com/doc/ 2004101l/leaver > .

McElroy, Robert W., "Why We Must Withdraw from Iraq: An Argument from Catholic Just-War Principles." *America* 30 Apr. 2007.

Oweiss, Ibrahim M., "Why Did the United States Fail in Its War on Iraq?" *Washington Report on Middle East Affairs* May–June 2007.

Pipes, Daniel, "Civil War in Iraq?" *New York Sun* 28 Feb. 2006.

"Plan for Quagmire," *Progressive* Jan. 2006: 8–11.

"Ret. Army General William Odom: U.S. Should 'Cut and Run' from Iraq," *Democracy Now.org* 4 Oct. 2005.

Sherman, Brad, "Hearing Before the Subcommittee on International Terrorism and Nonproliferation of the Committee on International Relations." House of Representatives, One Hundred Ninth Congress, Second Session, 11 May 2006 < www.foreignaffairs.house.gov/ archives/109/27478.pdf > .

Taibbi, Matt, "The Great Iraq Swindle." *Rolling Stone* Aug. 2007.

"The Terrorism Index," *Foreign Affairs* Sep.–Oct. 2007. < www.foreignpolicy.com/story/cms.php?story_id = 3924 > .

"Text of Al-Zarqawi Message Threatening More Attacks," *Federation of American Scientists* < www.fas.org/irp/ world/para/zarqawi040604.html > .

Web Sites

International Committee of the Red Cross (ICRC) Iraq Page (www.icrc.org/web/eng/siteeng0.nsf/htmlall/iraq?opend ocument&link = home). The ICRC, established in 1863, is an impartial, neutral, and independent international organization whose exclusively humanitarian mission is to protect the lives and dignity of victims of war and internal violence and to provide them with assistance. The ICRC is active in Iraq. Its Iraq page details its humanitarian efforts there.

International Federation of Red Cross and Red Crescent Societies (IFRC) Iraq Page (www.ifrc.org/where/country/cn6.asp?countryid = 87). The IFRC is the world's largest humanitarian organization, and its mission is to improve the lives of vulnerable people by mobilizing the power of humanity. IFRC is active in Iraq; its Iraq page describes its activities there and details the humanitarian crisis underway in that country.

Iraq Body Count (www.iraqbodycount.org). This Web site keeps track of how many civilians have died in the Iraq War. It draws from media reports, organization reports, hospital and morgue reports, and other official figures.

ReliefWeb Iraq (www.reliefweb.int). The ReliefWeb Iraq page contains the latest major documents and background information on humanitarian issues pertaining to Iraq.

U.N. High Commissioner for Refugees (UNHCR) (www.unhcr.org/cgi-bin/texis/vtx/home). This agency's purpose is to safeguard the rights and well-being of refugees. It coordinates efforts to protect refugees and resolve refugee problems worldwide. For information specifically on Iraq, click on the "Search Refworld" link below the search box and then select "Iraq" from the "Countries" drop-down menu.

U.S. Embassy in Iraq (http://iraq.usembassy.gov/). This Web site provides current information pertaining to the new sovereign Iraq, which includes "Key Embassy Links" and other useful information concerning Iraq.

World Health Organization (WHO) Iraq Country Page (www.who.int/countries/irq/en/). The World Health Organization is the United Nations' specialized agency for health. Its Iraq page monitors health crises in Iraq, including outbreaks of disease and quality of life conditions that result in degraded health.

Index

Picture Credits

About the Editor

Lauri S. Friedman earned her bachelor's degree in religion and political science from Vassar College in Poughkeepsie, NY. Her studies there focused on political Islam. Friedman has worked as a non-fiction writer, a newspaper journalist, and an editor for more than 8 years. She has accumulated extensive experience in both academic and professional settings.

Friedman is the founder of LSF Editorial, a writing and editing outfit in San Diego. Her clients include Greenhaven Press, for whom she has edited and authored numerous publications on controversial social issues such as gay marriage, prisons, genetically modified food, racism, suicide bombers, and the drug abuse. Much of the *Writing the Critical Essay* series has been under her direction or authorship. She was instrumental in the creation of the series, and played a critical role in its conception and development.